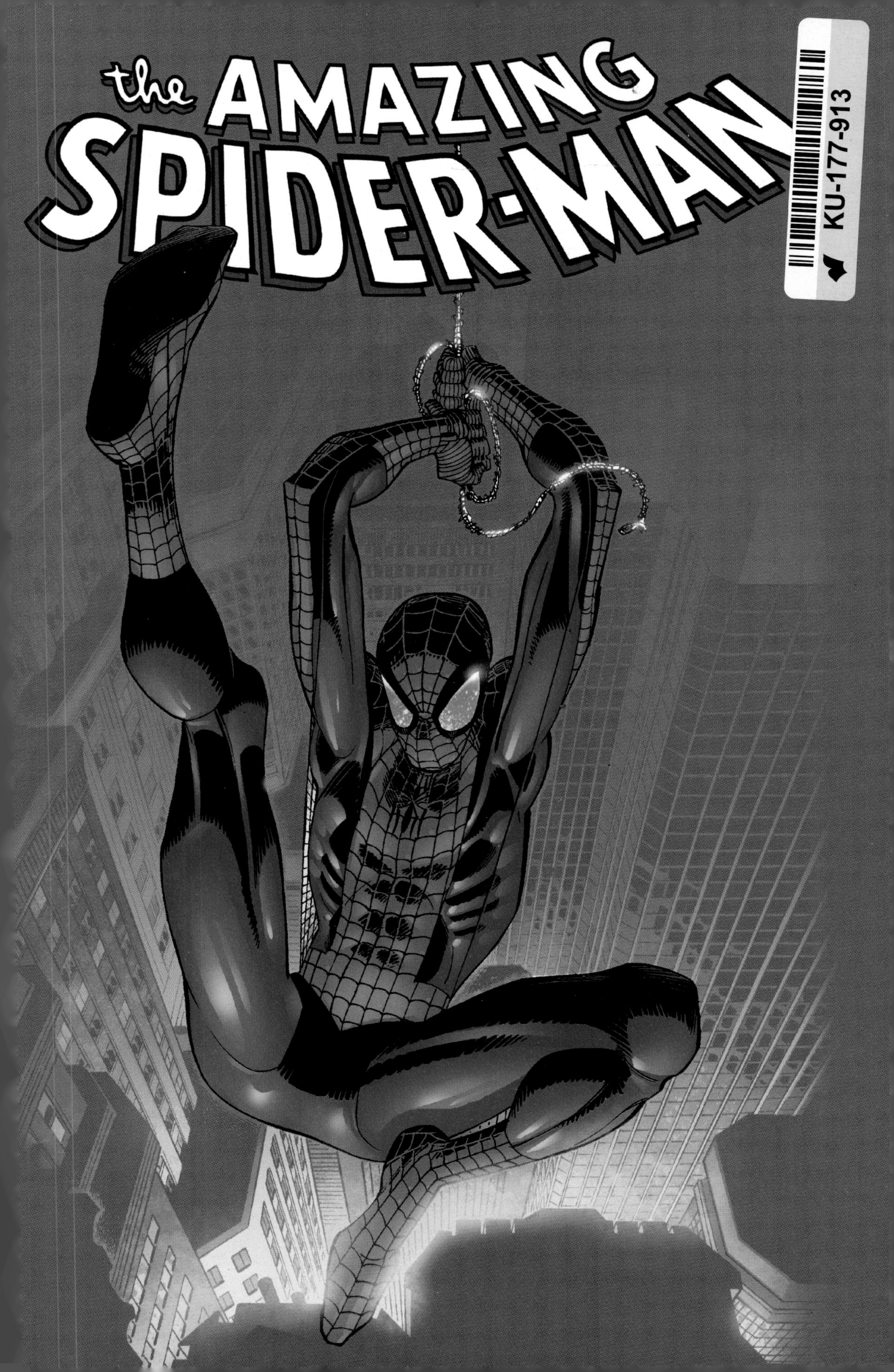
the AMAZING
SPIDER-MAN

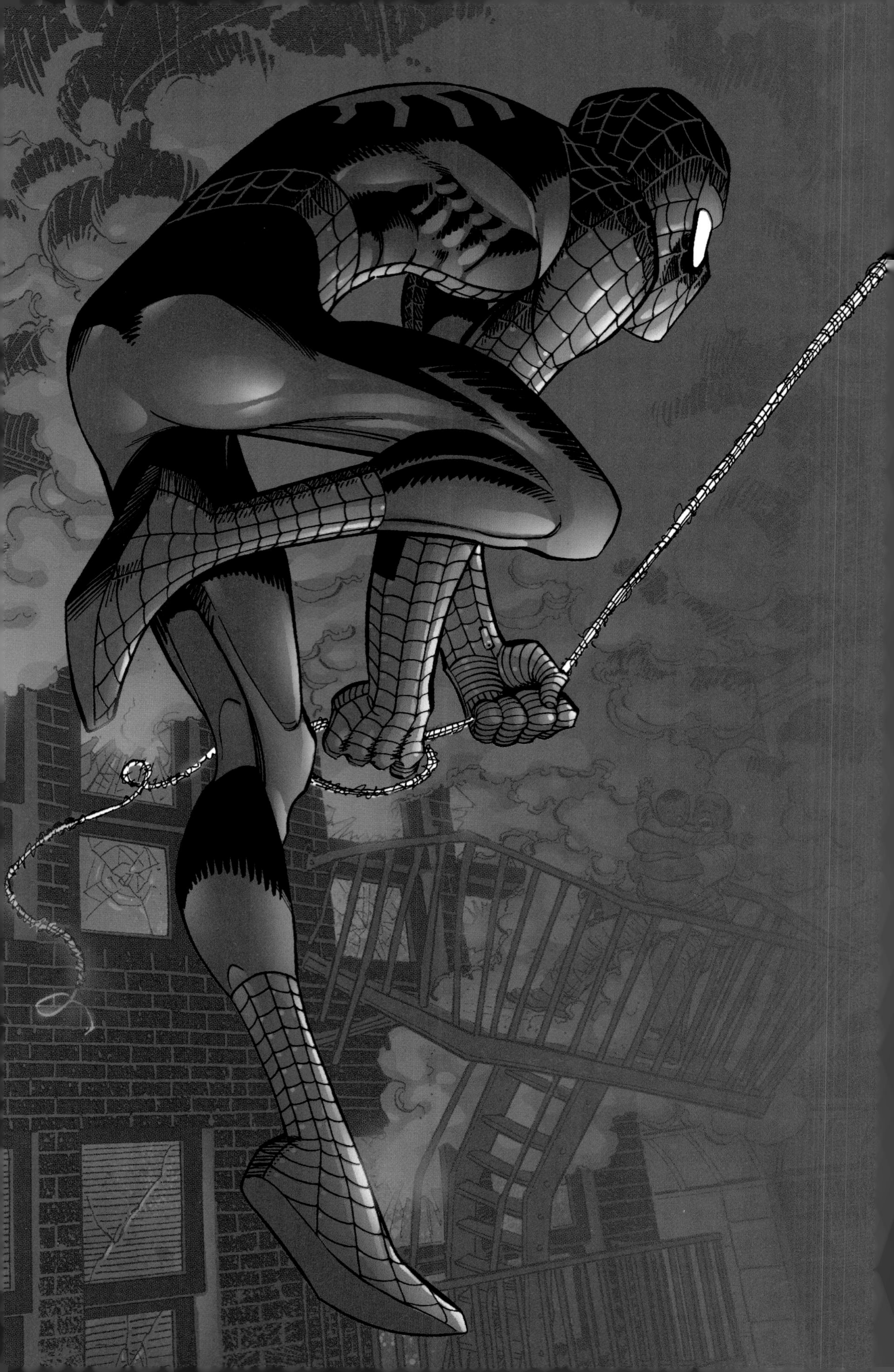

the AMAZING SPIDER-MAN

REVELATIONS

WRITTEN BY
J. MICHAEL STRACZYNSKI

PENCILS
JOHN ROMITA JR.

INKS
SCOTT HANNA

COLORS
DAN KEMP & AVALON STUDIOS

LETTERS
RS & COMICRAFT'S WES ABBOTT

COVER
KAARE ANDREWS

ASSISTANT EDITOR
JOHN MIESEGAES

EDITOR
AXEL ALONSO

EDITOR IN CHIEF
JOE QUESADA

PRESIDENT
BILL JEMAS

AMAZING SPIDER-MAN VOL. 2: REVELATIONS. Contains material originally published in magazine form as AMAZING SPIDER-MAN (Vol. 2) #36-39 . Second printing 2002. ISBN# 0-7851-0877-7. Published by MARVEL COMICS, a division of MARVEL ENTERTAINMENT GROUP, INC. OFFICE OF PUBLICATION: 10 East 40th Street, New York, NY 10016. Copyright © 2001 and 2002 Marvel Characters, Inc. All rights reserved. $8.99 per copy in the U.S. and $14.50 in Canada (GST #R127032852); Canadian Agreement #40668537. All characters featured in this issue and the distinctive names and likenesses thereof, and all related indicia are trademarks of Marvel Characters, Inc. No similarity between any of the names, characters, persons, and/or institutions in this magazine with those of any living or dead person or institution is intended, and any such similarity which may exist is purely coincidental. **Printed in Canada.** STAN LEE, Chairman Emeritus. For information regarding advertising in Marvel Comics or on Marvel.com, please contact Russell Brown, Executive Vice President, Consumer Products, Promotions and Media Sales at 212-576-8561 or rbrown@marvel.com

10 9 8 7 6 5 4 3 2

We interrupt our regularly
scheduled program to bring you
the following Special Bulletin.

LONGITUDE: 74 DEGREES,
0 MINUTES, 23 SECONDS WEST.
LATITUDE: 40 DEGREES,
42 MINUTES, 51 SECONDS NORTH.

FOLLOW THE SOUND
OF SIRENS...

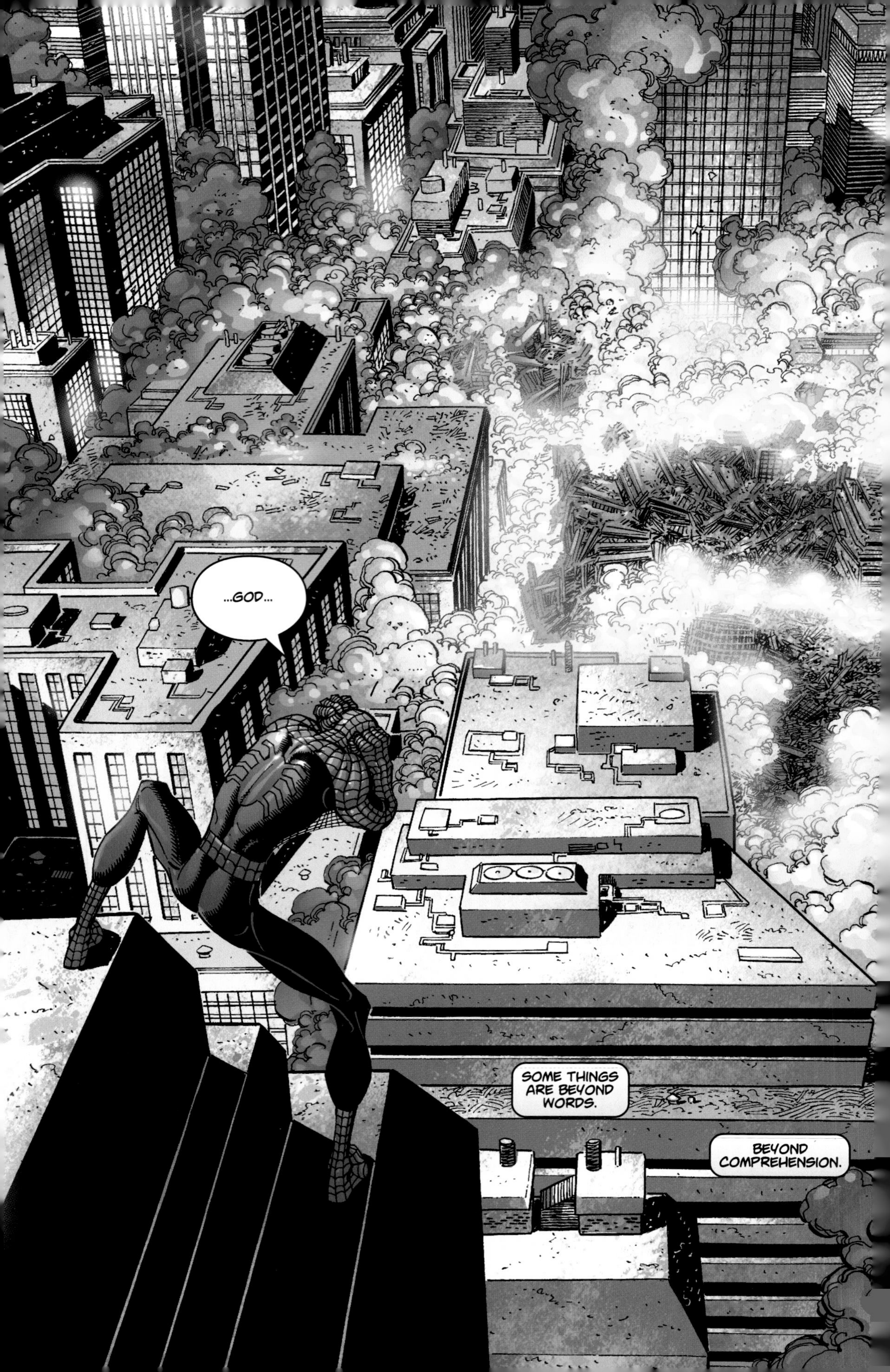
...GOD...
SOME THINGS ARE BEYOND WORDS.
BEYOND COMPREHENSION.

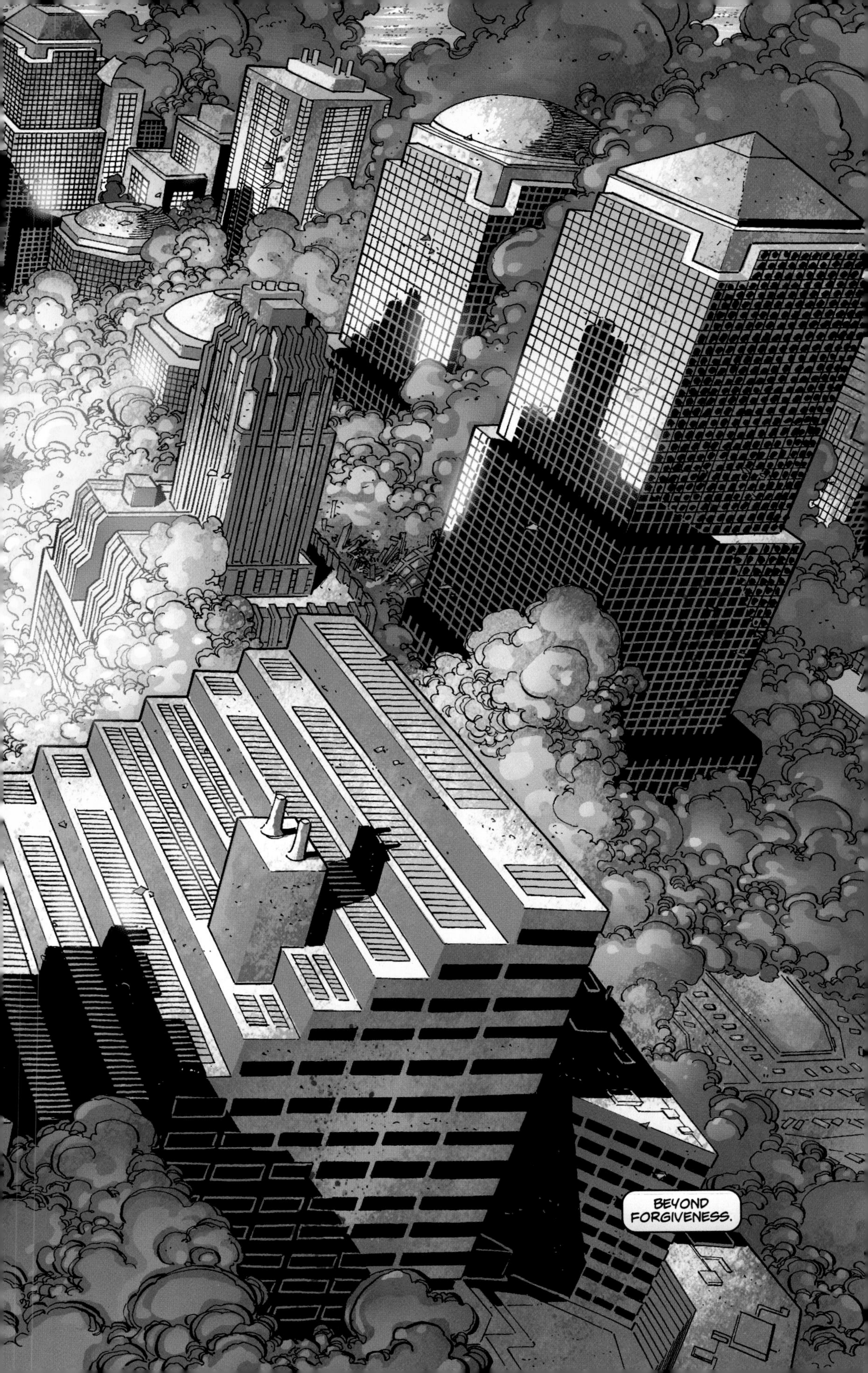
BEYOND
FORGIVENESS.

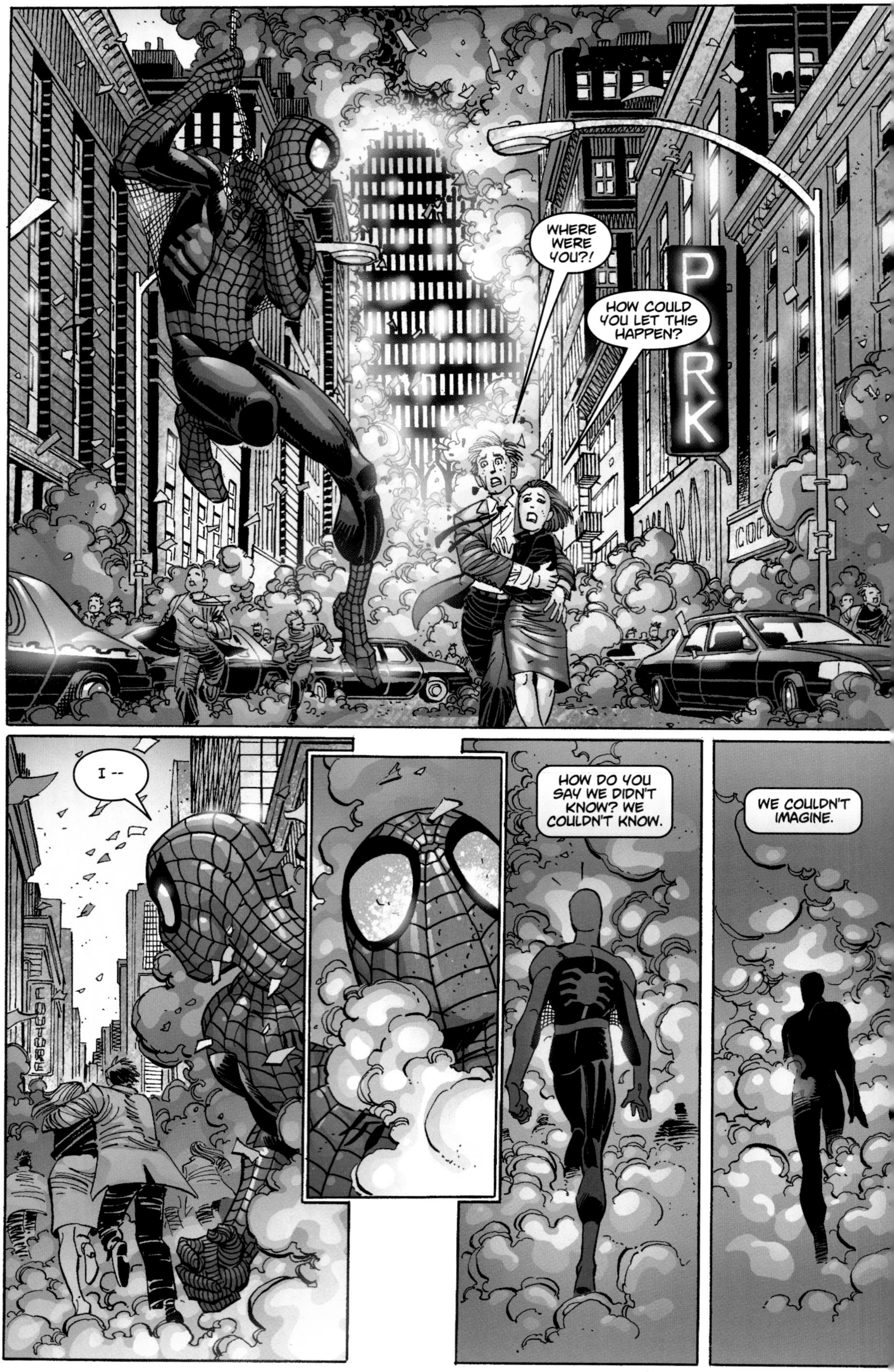
WHERE WERE YOU?!
HOW COULD YOU LET THIS HAPPEN?
PARK
I --
HOW DO YOU SAY WE DIDN'T KNOW? WE COULDN'T KNOW.
WE COULDN'T IMAGINE.

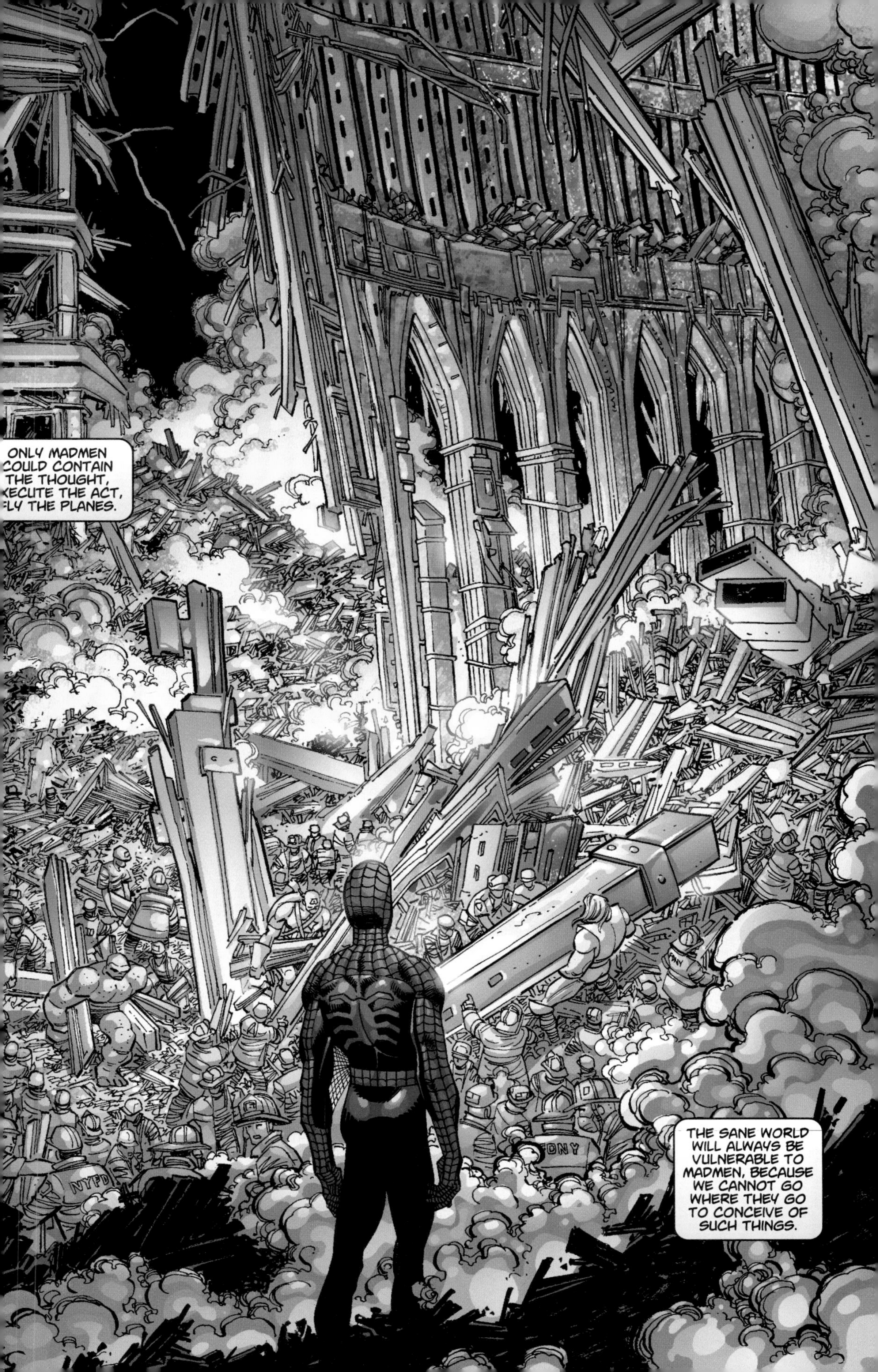
ONLY MADMEN COULD CONTAIN THE THOUGHT, XECUTE THE ACT, FLY THE PLANES.
THE SANE WORLD WILL ALWAYS BE VULNERABLE TO MADMEN, BECAUSE WE CANNOT GO WHERE THEY GO TO CONCEIVE OF SUCH THINGS.
NYPD
FDNY

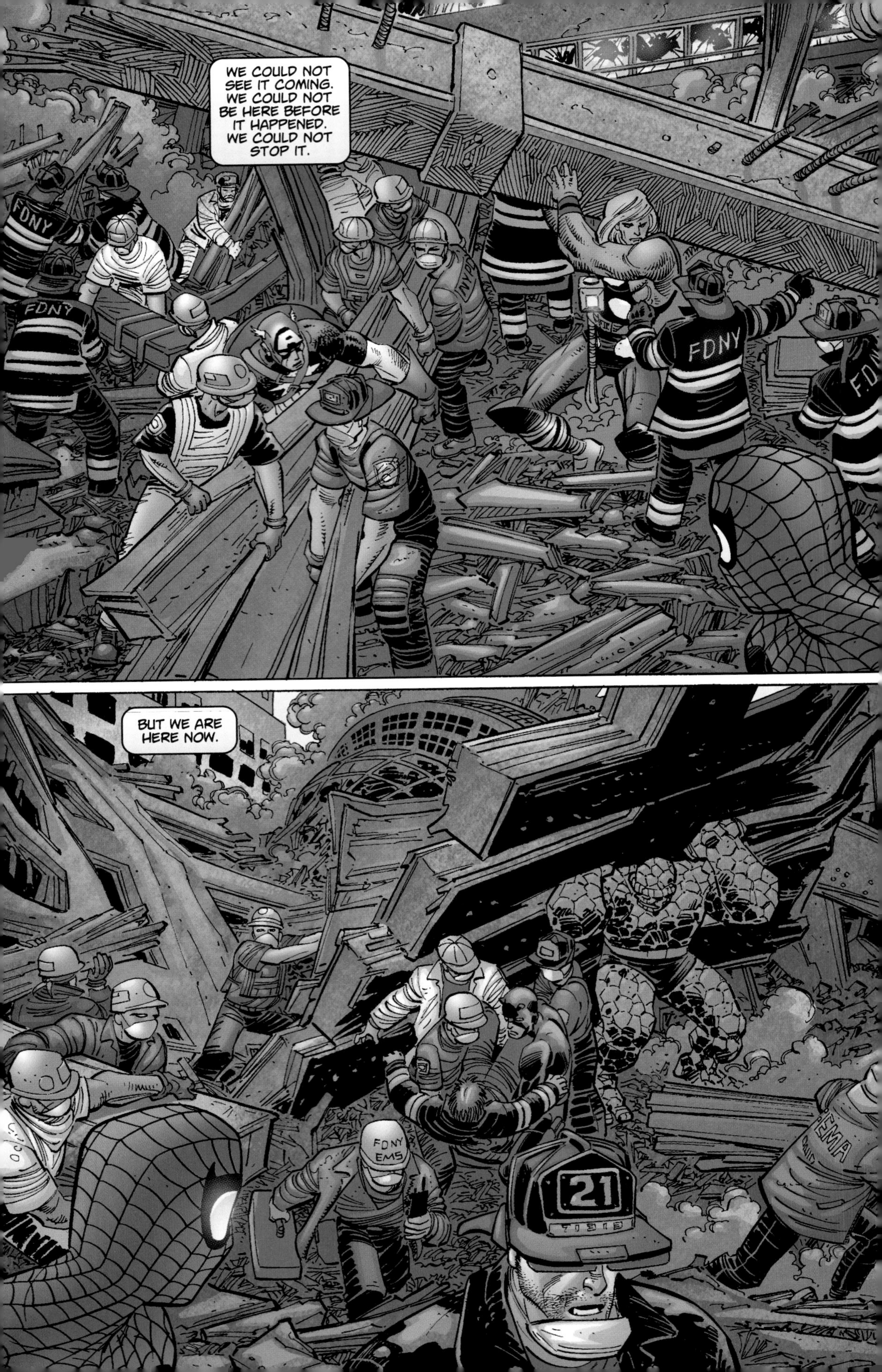
WE COULD NOT SEE IT COMING. WE COULD NOT BE HERE BEFORE IT HAPPENED. WE COULD NOT STOP IT.
FDNY
FDNY
NYPD
FDNY
BUT WE ARE HERE NOW.
FDNY EMS
21
FEMA

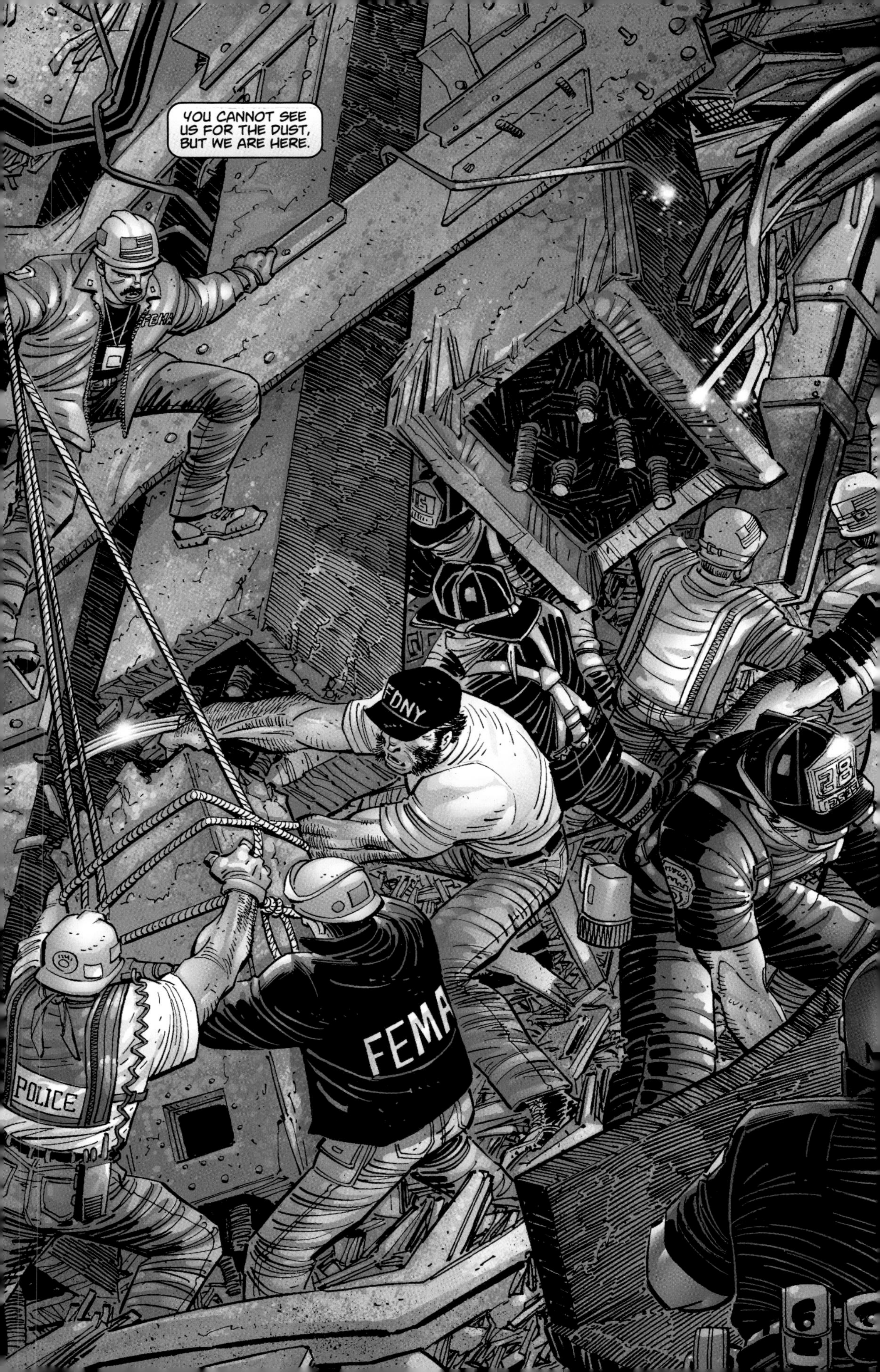
YOU CANNOT SEE US FOR THE DUST, BUT WE ARE HERE.
FEMA
FDNY
FEMA
POLICE
28

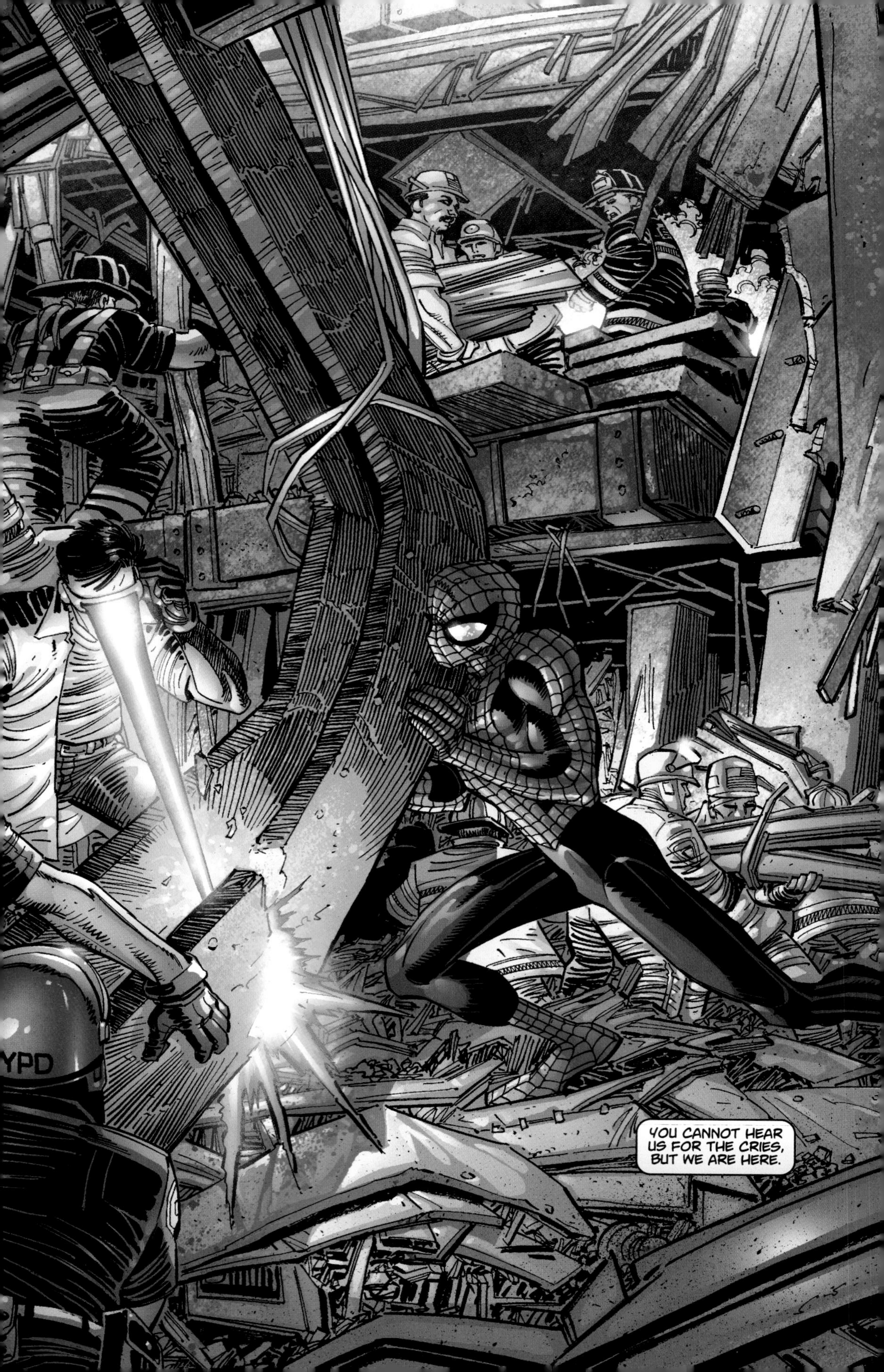
YPD
YOU CANNOT HEAR US FOR THE CRIES, BUT WE ARE HERE.

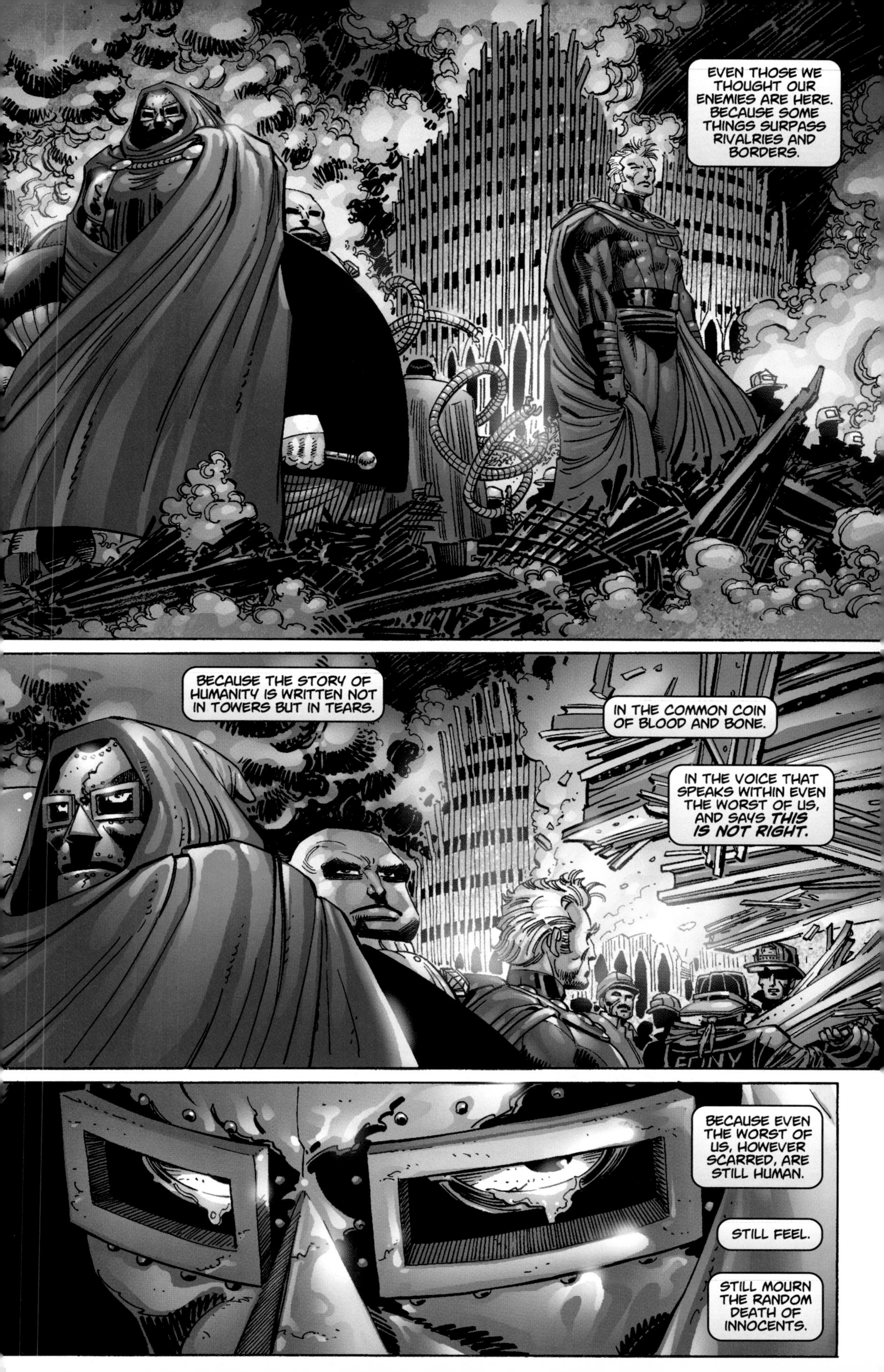
EVEN THOSE WE THOUGHT OUR ENEMIES ARE HERE. BECAUSE SOME THINGS SURPASS RIVALRIES AND BORDERS.
BECAUSE THE STORY OF HUMANITY IS WRITTEN NOT IN TOWERS BUT IN TEARS.
IN THE COMMON COIN OF BLOOD AND BONE.
IN THE VOICE THAT SPEAKS WITHIN EVEN THE WORST OF US, AND SAYS *THIS IS NOT RIGHT.*
BECAUSE EVEN THE WORST OF US, HOWEVER SCARRED, ARE STILL HUMAN.
STILL FEEL.
STILL MOURN THE RANDOM DEATH OF INNOCENTS.

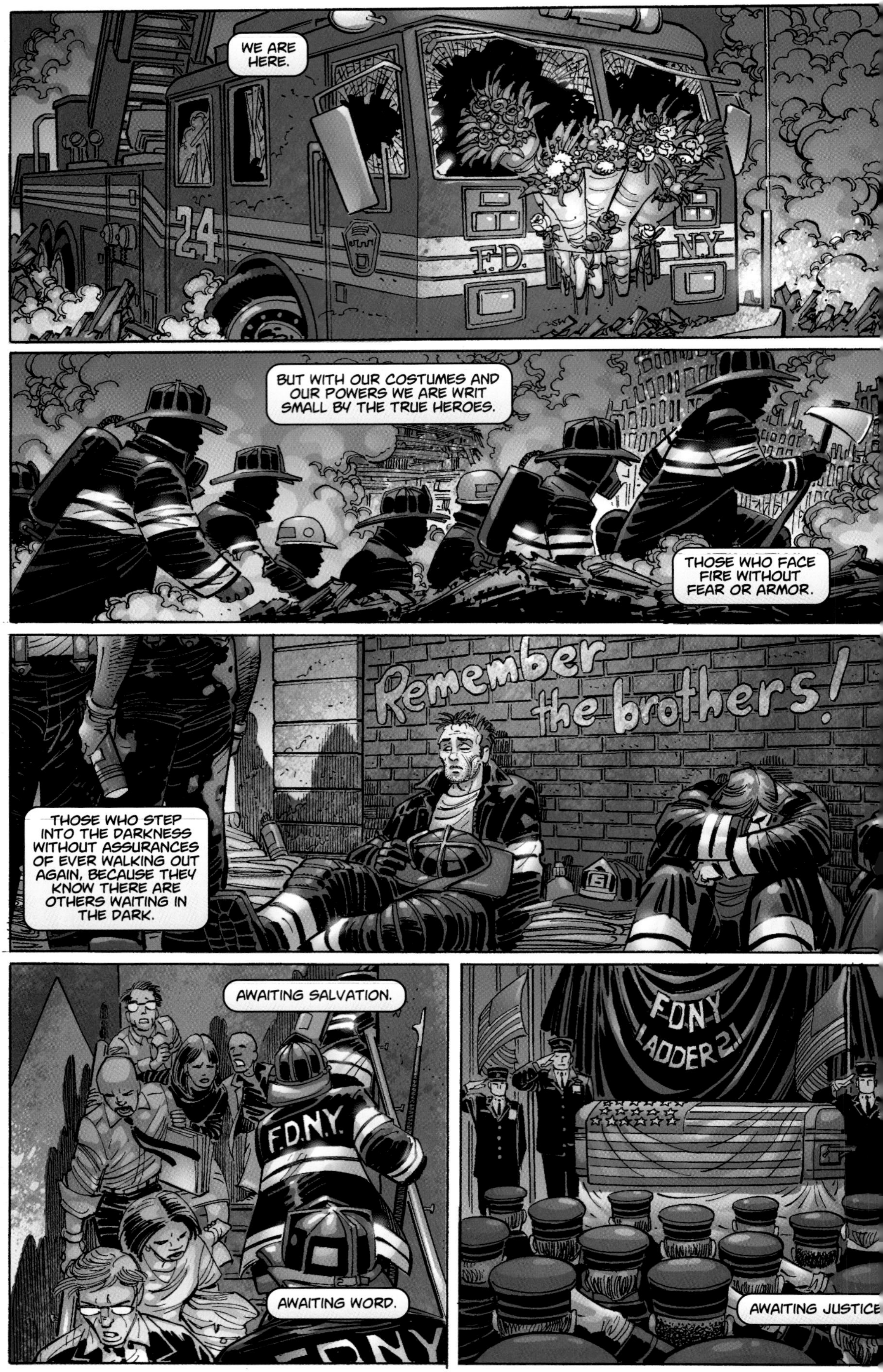
WE ARE HERE.
F.D.
N.Y.
24
BUT WITH OUR COSTUMES AND OUR POWERS WE ARE WRIT SMALL BY THE TRUE HEROES.
THOSE WHO FACE FIRE WITHOUT FEAR OR ARMOR.
Remember the brothers!
THOSE WHO STEP INTO THE DARKNESS WITHOUT ASSURANCES OF EVER WALKING OUT AGAIN, BECAUSE THEY KNOW THERE ARE OTHERS WAITING IN THE DARK.
AWAITING SALVATION.
F.D.N.Y.
AWAITING WORD.
F.D.N.Y
LADDER 21
AWAITING JUSTICE

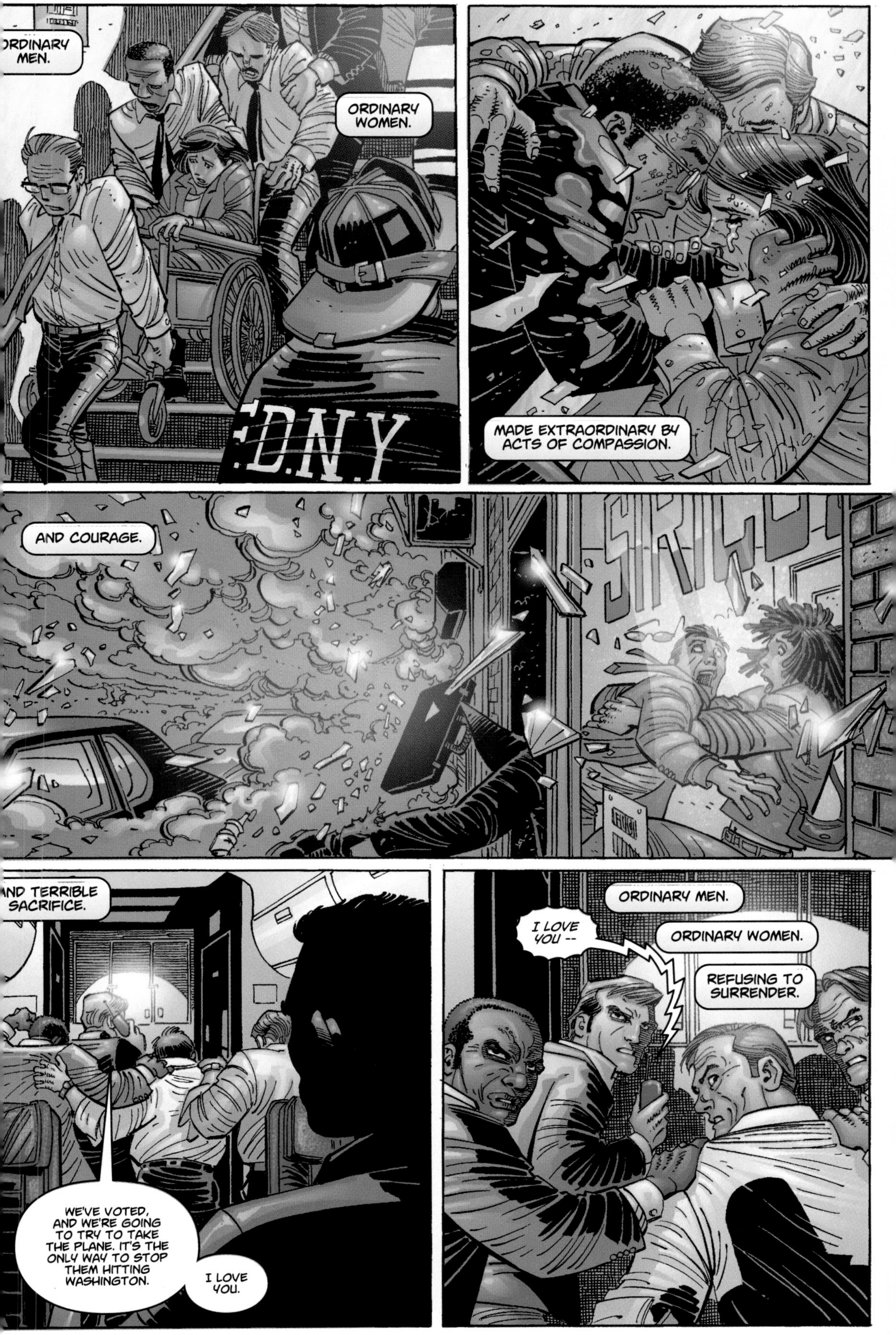
ORDINARY MEN.
ORDINARY WOMEN.
F.D.N.Y
MADE EXTRAORDINARY BY ACTS OF COMPASSION.
AND COURAGE.
AND TERRIBLE SACRIFICE.
WE'VE VOTED, AND WE'RE GOING TO TRY TO TAKE THE PLANE. IT'S THE ONLY WAY TO STOP THEM HITTING WASHINGTON.
I LOVE YOU.
ORDINARY MEN.
I LOVE YOU --
ORDINARY WOMEN.
REFUSING TO SURRENDER.

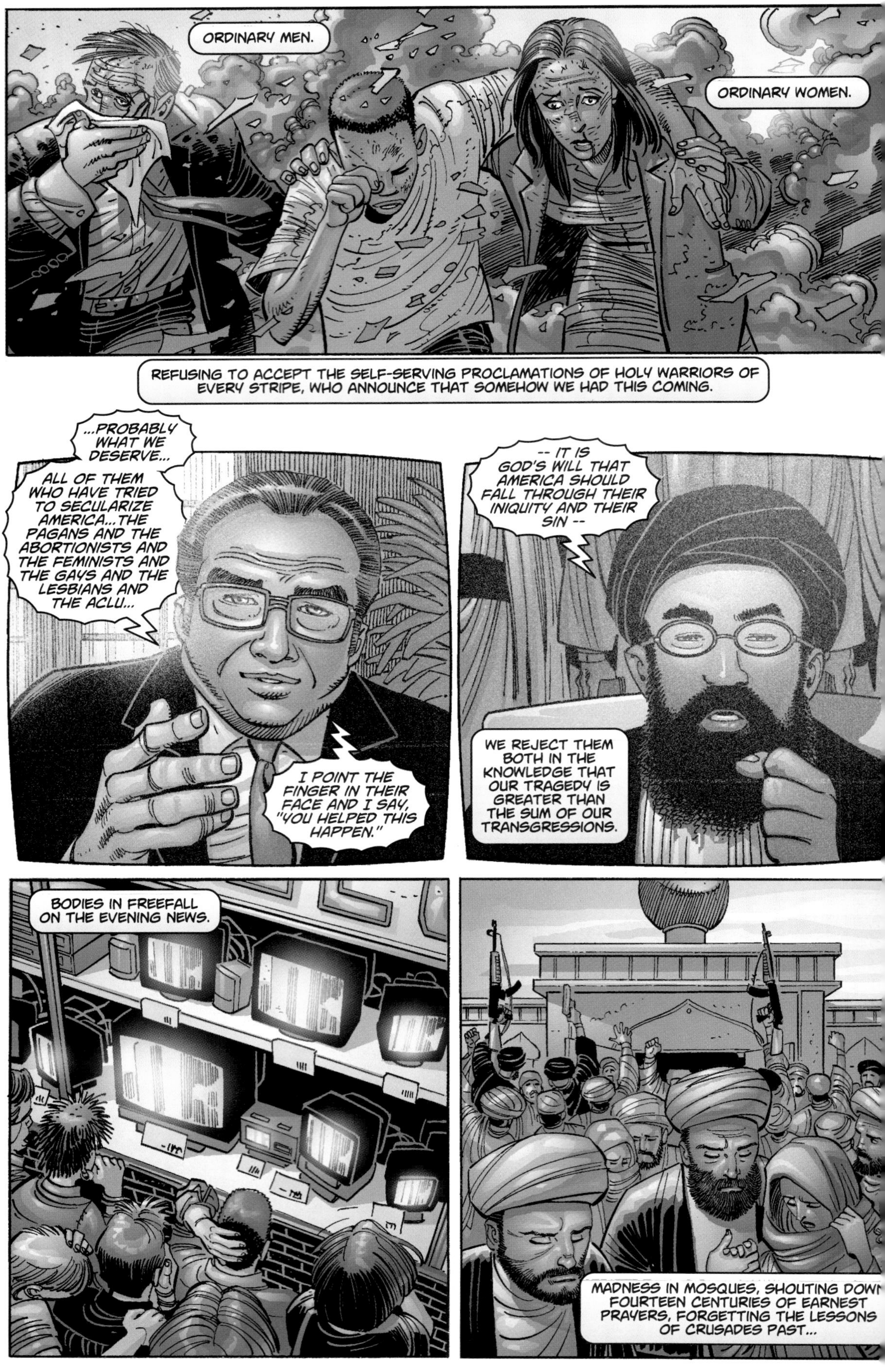
ORDINARY MEN.
ORDINARY WOMEN.
REFUSING TO ACCEPT THE SELF-SERVING PROCLAMATIONS OF HOLY WARRIORS OF EVERY STRIPE, WHO ANNOUNCE THAT SOMEHOW WE HAD THIS COMING.
...PROBABLY WHAT WE DESERVE...
ALL OF THEM WHO HAVE TRIED TO SECULARIZE AMERICA...THE PAGANS AND THE ABORTIONISTS AND THE FEMINISTS AND THE GAYS AND THE LESBIANS AND THE ACLU...
I POINT THE FINGER IN THEIR FACE AND I SAY, "YOU HELPED THIS HAPPEN."
-- IT IS GOD'S WILL THAT AMERICA SHOULD FALL THROUGH THEIR INIQUITY AND THEIR SIN --
WE REJECT THEM BOTH IN THE KNOWLEDGE THAT OUR TRAGEDY IS GREATER THAN THE SUM OF OUR TRANSGRESSIONS.
BODIES IN FREEFALL ON THE EVENING NEWS.
MADNESS IN MOSQUES, SHOUTING DOWN FOURTEEN CENTURIES OF EARNEST PRAYERS, FORGETTING THE LESSONS OF CRUSADES PAST...

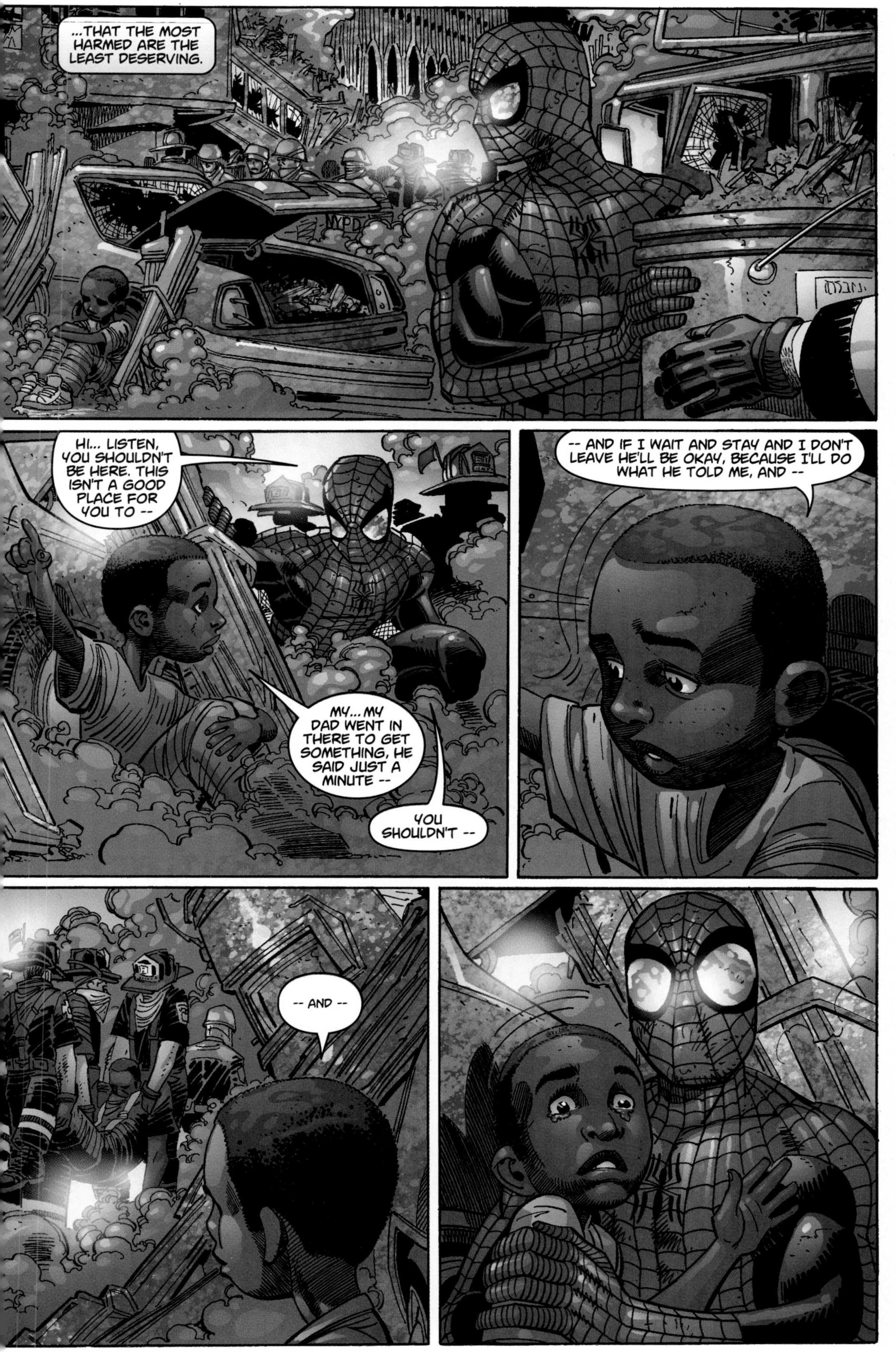
...THAT THE MOST HARMED ARE THE LEAST DESERVING.
NYPD
HI... LISTEN, YOU SHOULDN'T BE HERE. THIS ISN'T A GOOD PLACE FOR YOU TO --
MY... MY DAD WENT IN THERE TO GET SOMETHING, HE SAID JUST A MINUTE --
YOU SHOULDN'T --
-- AND IF I WAIT AND STAY AND I DON'T LEAVE HE'LL BE OKAY, BECAUSE I'LL DO WHAT HE TOLD ME, AND --
-- AND --

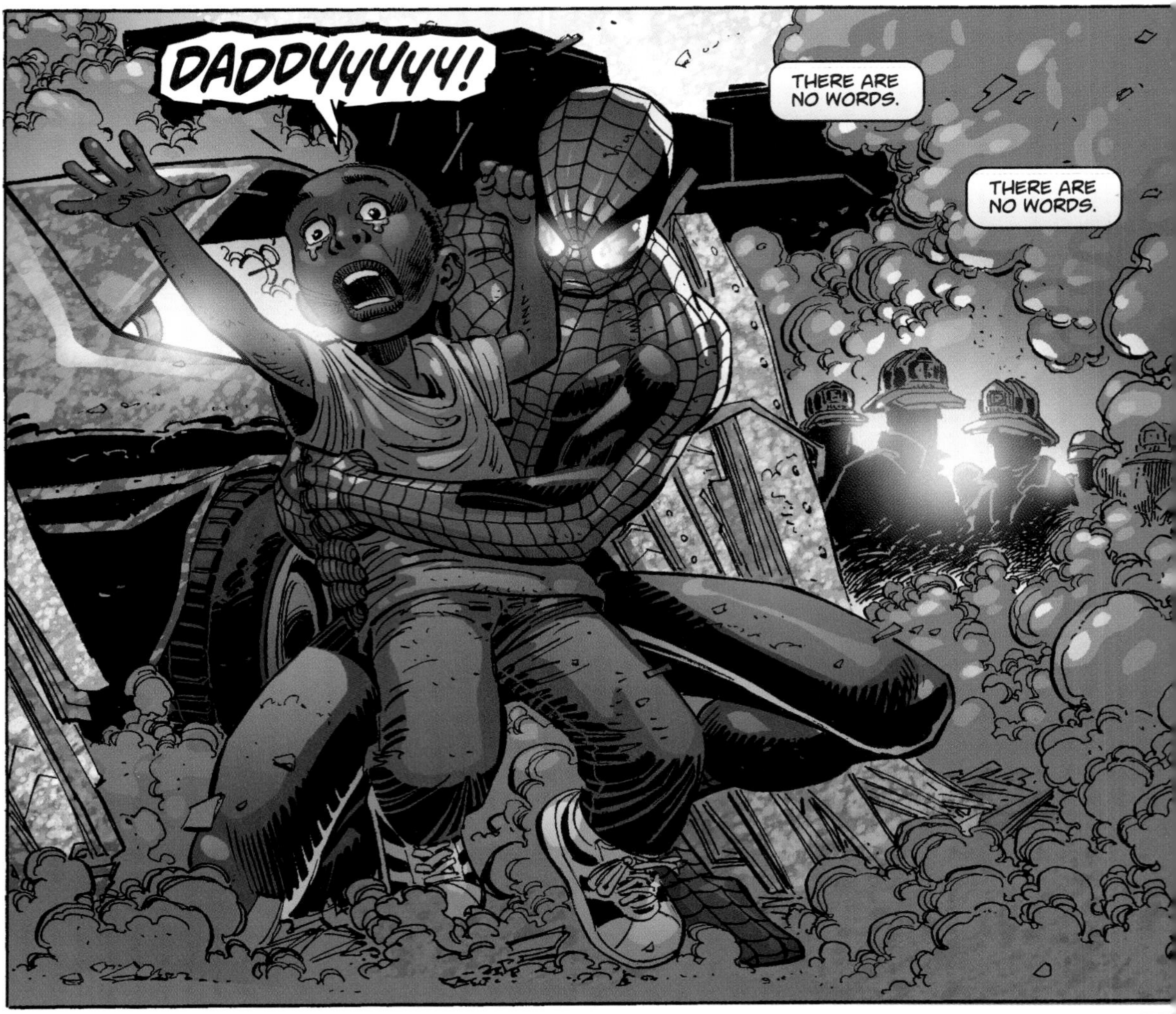
DADDYYYYY!
THERE ARE NO WORDS.
THERE ARE NO WORDS.

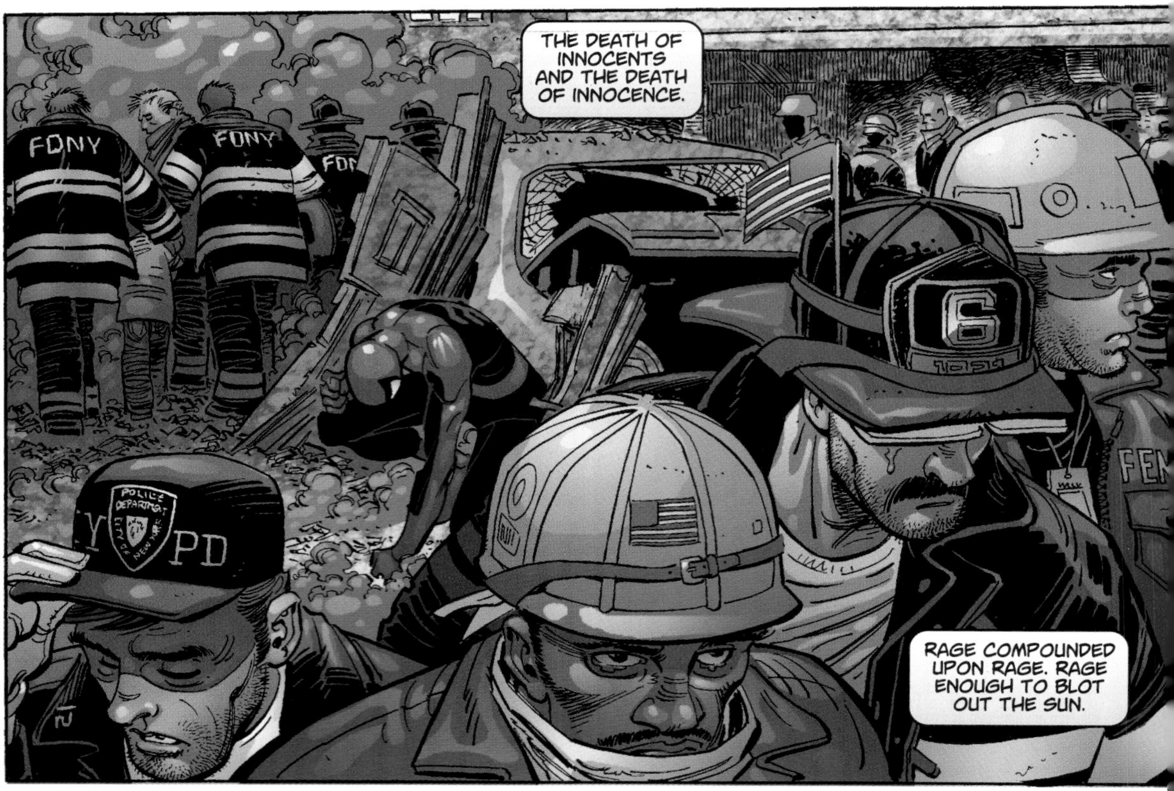
THE DEATH OF INNOCENTS AND THE DEATH OF INNOCENCE.
FDNY
FDNY
NYPD
RAGE COMPOUNDED UPON RAGE. RAGE ENOUGH TO BLOT OUT THE SUN.

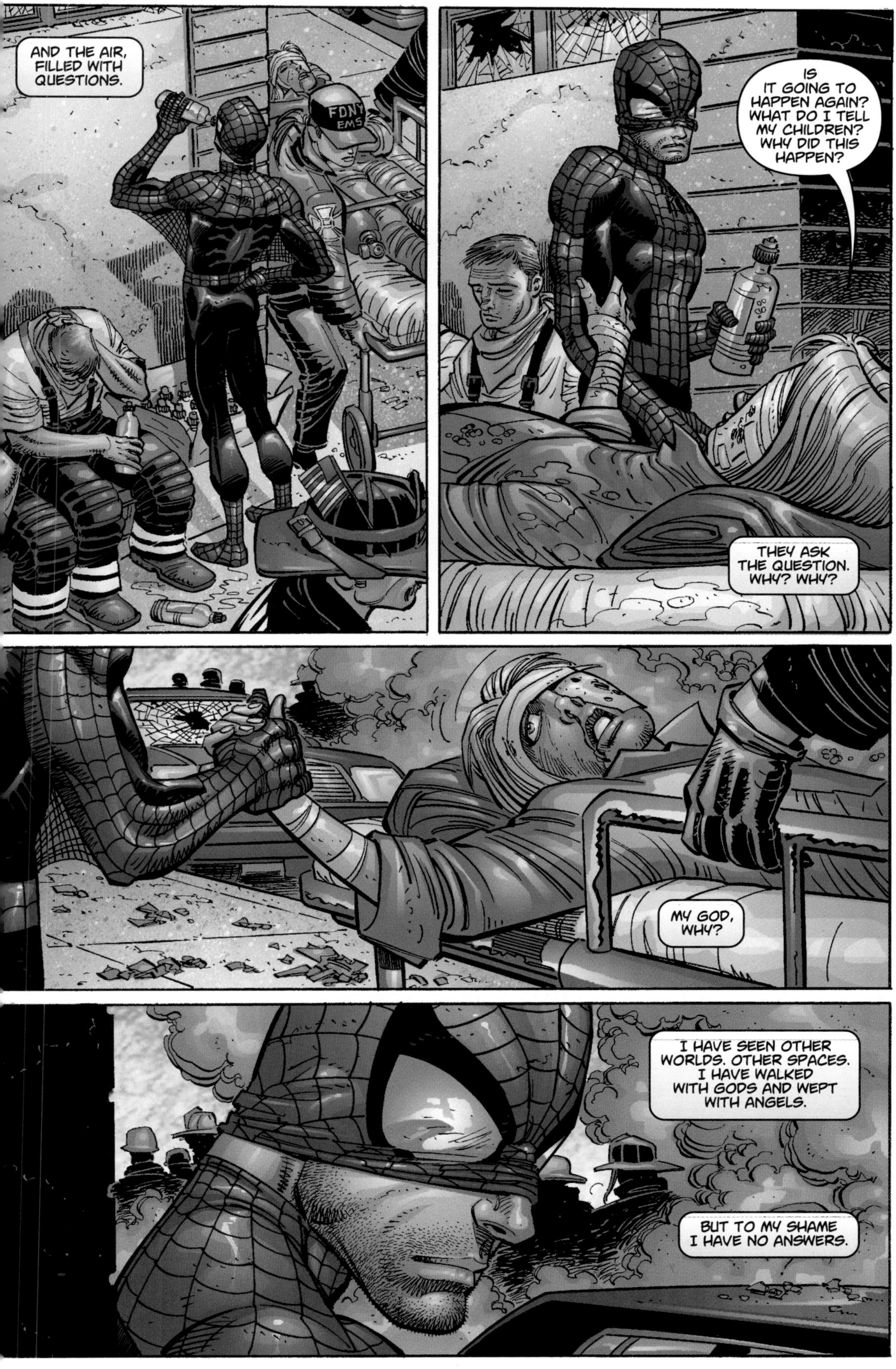
AND THE AIR, FILLED WITH QUESTIONS.
FDNY EMS
IS IT GOING TO HAPPEN AGAIN? WHAT DO I TELL MY CHILDREN? WHY DID THIS HAPPEN?
THEY ASK THE QUESTION. WHY? WHY?
MY GOD, WHY?
I HAVE SEEN OTHER WORLDS. OTHER SPACES. I HAVE WALKED WITH GODS AND WEPT WITH ANGELS.
BUT TO MY SHAME I HAVE NO ANSWERS.

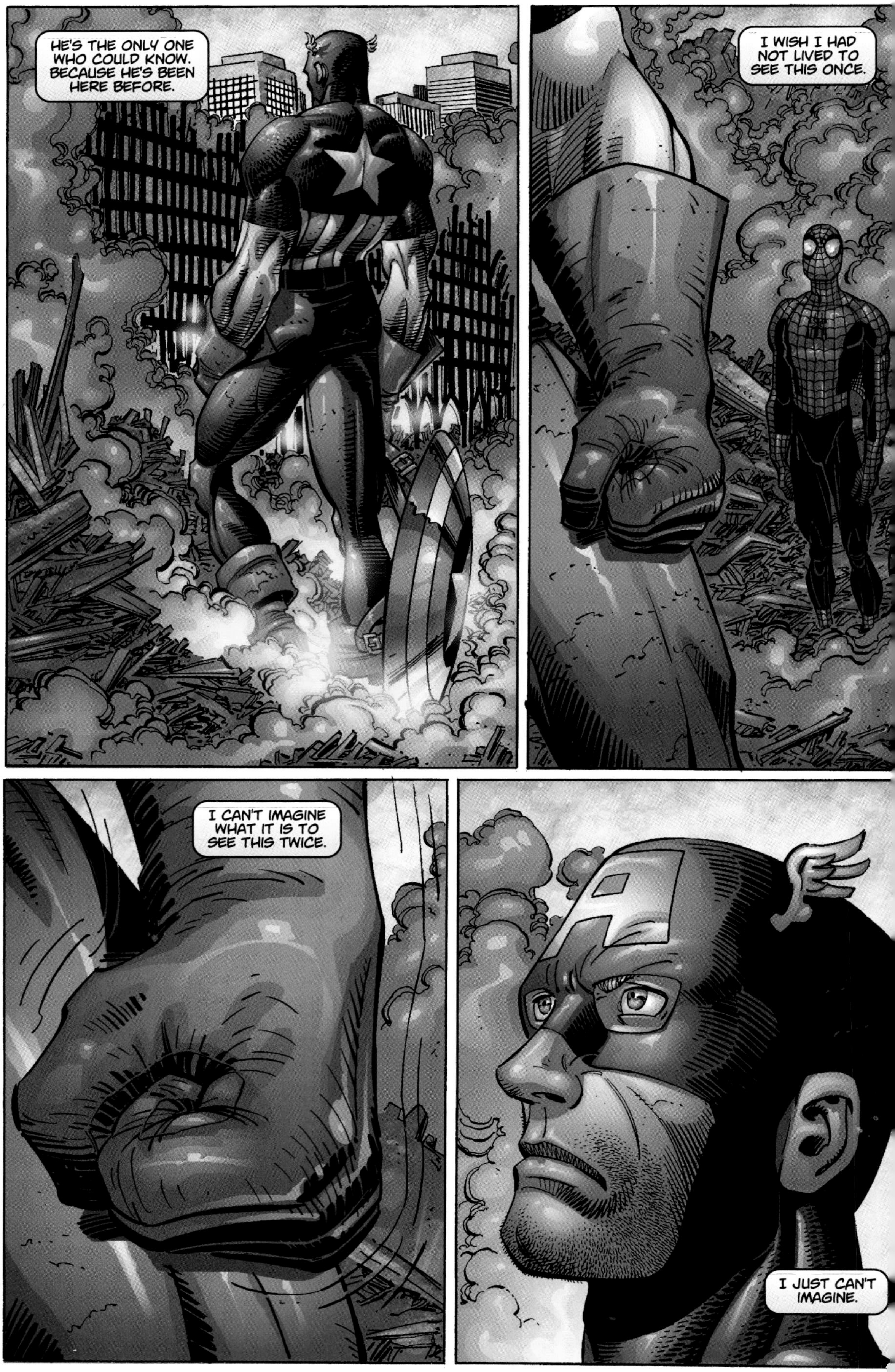
HE'S THE ONLY ONE WHO COULD KNOW. BECAUSE HE'S BEEN HERE BEFORE.
I WISH I HAD NOT LIVED TO SEE THIS ONCE.
I CAN'T IMAGINE WHAT IT IS TO SEE THIS TWICE.
I JUST CAN'T IMAGINE.

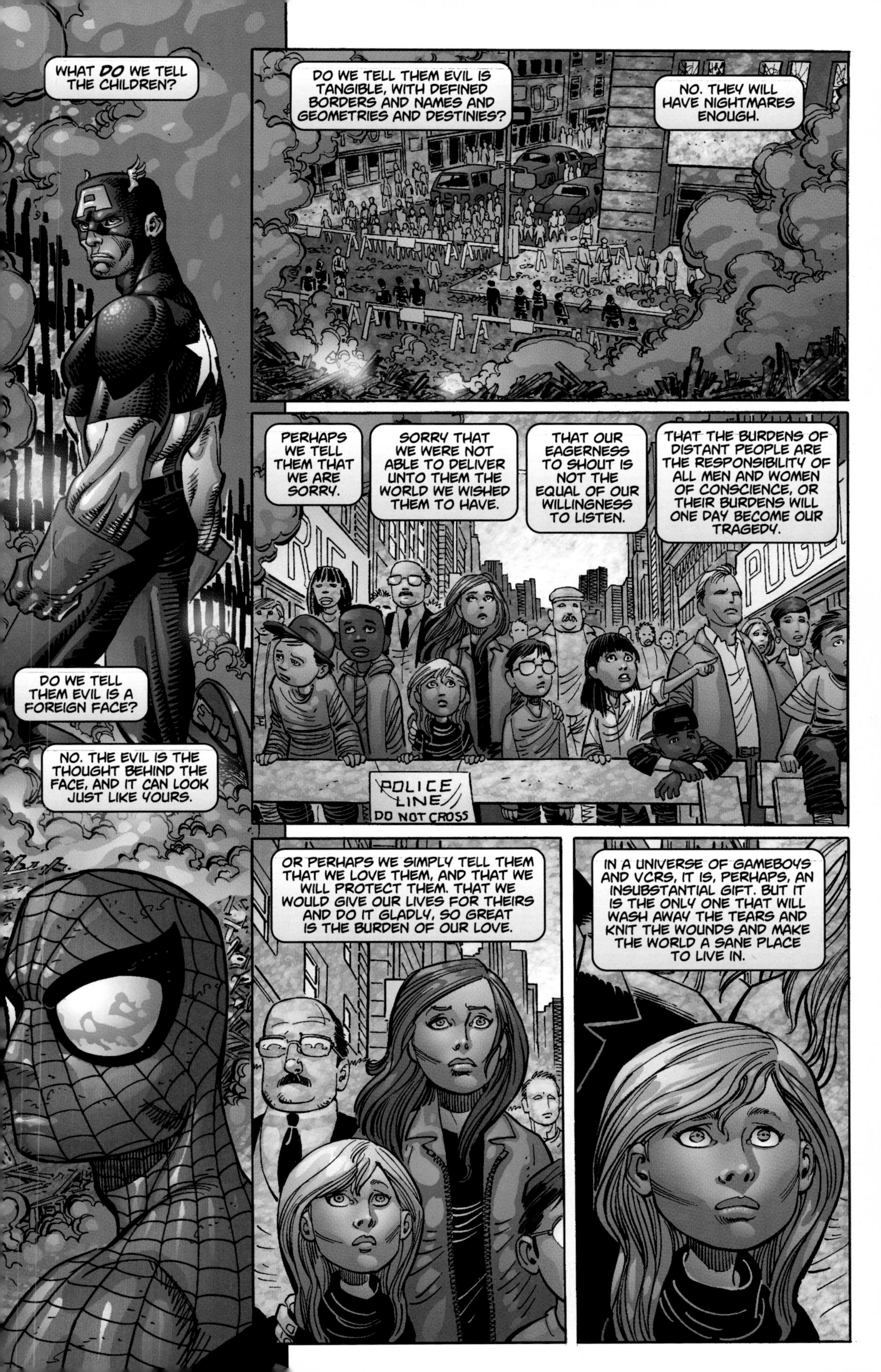
WHAT DO WE TELL THE CHILDREN?
DO WE TELL THEM EVIL IS TANGIBLE, WITH DEFINED BORDERS AND NAMES AND GEOMETRIES AND DESTINIES?
NO. THEY WILL HAVE NIGHTMARES ENOUGH.
DO WE TELL THEM EVIL IS A FOREIGN FACE?
NO. THE EVIL IS THE THOUGHT BEHIND THE FACE, AND IT CAN LOOK JUST LIKE YOURS.
PERHAPS WE TELL THEM THAT WE ARE SORRY.
SORRY THAT WE WERE NOT ABLE TO DELIVER UNTO THEM THE WORLD WE WISHED THEM TO HAVE.
THAT OUR EAGERNESS TO SHOUT IS NOT THE EQUAL OF OUR WILLINGNESS TO LISTEN.
THAT THE BURDENS OF DISTANT PEOPLE ARE THE RESPONSIBILITY OF ALL MEN AND WOMEN OF CONSCIENCE, OR THEIR BURDENS WILL ONE DAY BECOME OUR TRAGEDY.
POLICE LINE DO NOT CROSS
OR PERHAPS WE SIMPLY TELL THEM THAT WE LOVE THEM, AND THAT WE WILL PROTECT THEM. THAT WE WOULD GIVE OUR LIVES FOR THEIRS AND DO IT GLADLY, SO GREAT IS THE BURDEN OF OUR LOVE.
IN A UNIVERSE OF GAMEBOYS AND VCRS, IT IS, PERHAPS, AN INSUBSTANTIAL GIFT. BUT IT IS THE ONLY ONE THAT WILL WASH AWAY THE TEARS AND KNIT THE WOUNDS AND MAKE THE WORLD A SANE PLACE TO LIVE IN.

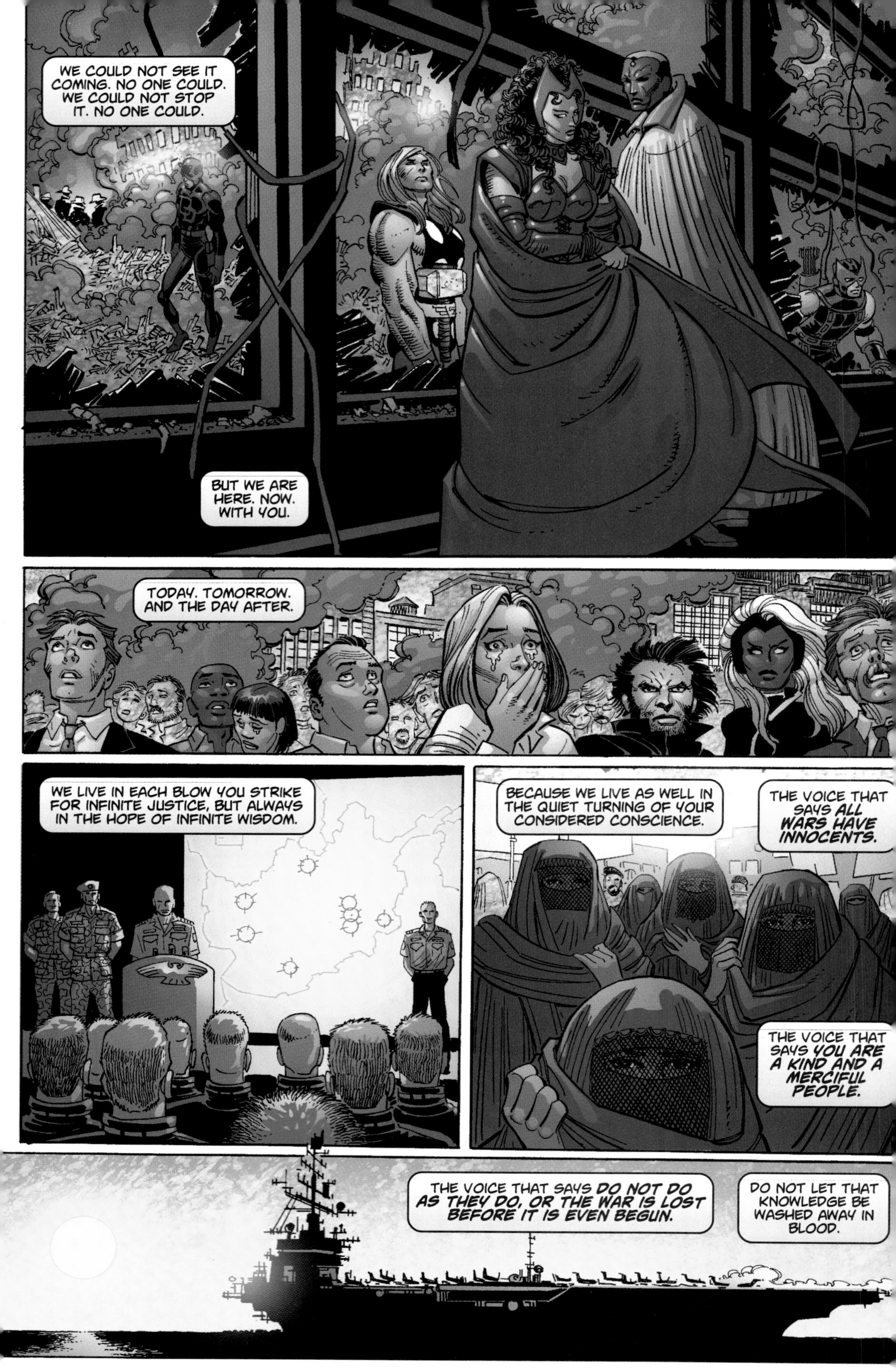
WE COULD NOT SEE IT COMING. NO ONE COULD. WE COULD NOT STOP IT. NO ONE COULD.
BUT WE ARE HERE. NOW. WITH YOU.
TODAY. TOMORROW. AND THE DAY AFTER.
WE LIVE IN EACH BLOW YOU STRIKE FOR INFINITE JUSTICE, BUT ALWAYS IN THE HOPE OF INFINITE WISDOM.
BECAUSE WE LIVE AS WELL IN THE QUIET TURNING OF YOUR CONSIDERED CONSCIENCE.
THE VOICE THAT SAYS ALL WARS HAVE INNOCENTS.
THE VOICE THAT SAYS YOU ARE A KIND AND A MERCIFUL PEOPLE.
THE VOICE THAT SAYS DO NOT DO AS THEY DO, OR THE WAR IS LOST BEFORE IT IS EVEN BEGUN.
DO NOT LET THAT KNOWLEDGE BE WASHED AWAY IN BLOOD.

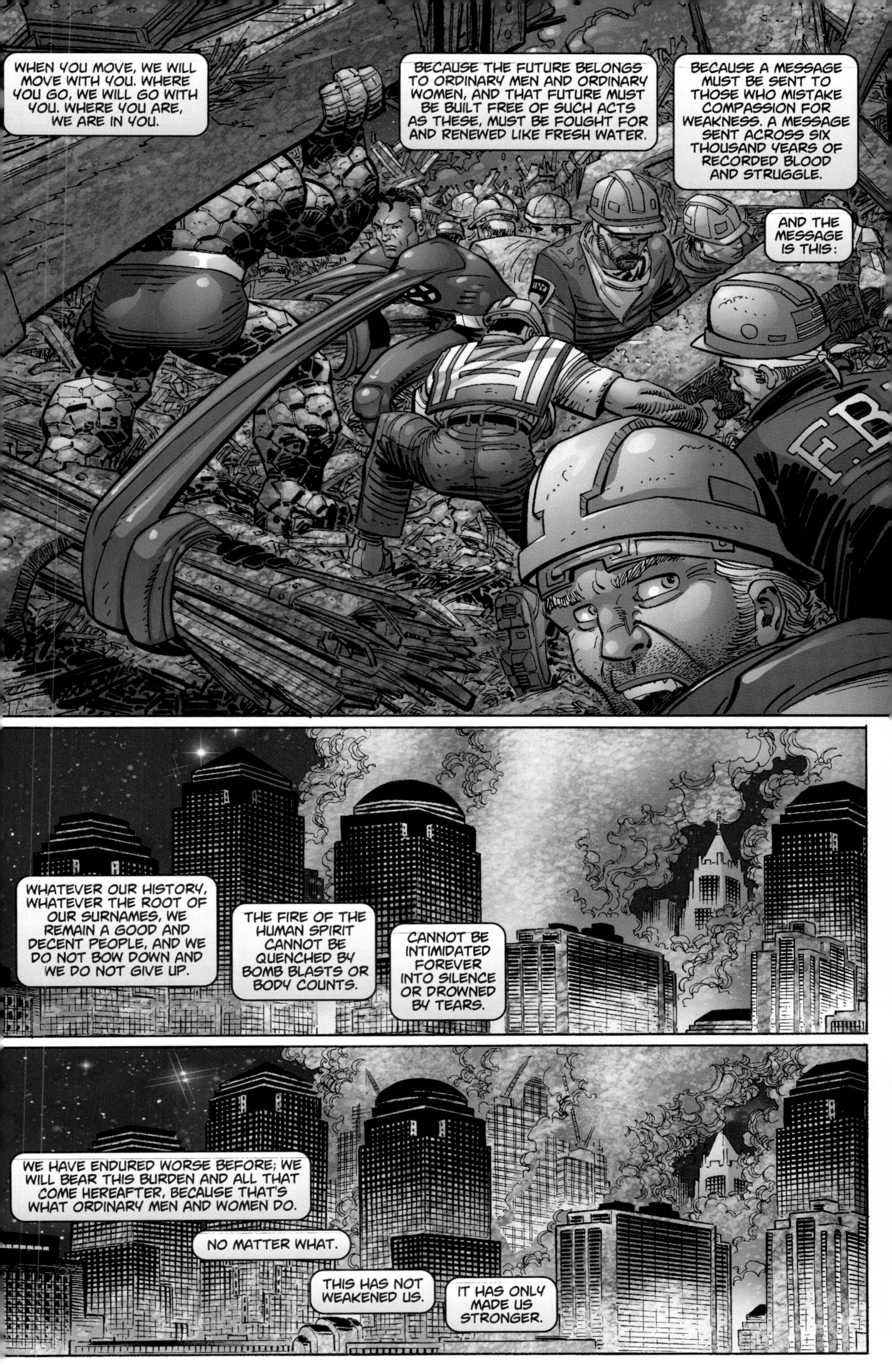
WHEN YOU MOVE, WE WILL MOVE WITH YOU. WHERE YOU GO, WE WILL GO WITH YOU. WHERE YOU ARE, WE ARE IN YOU.
BECAUSE THE FUTURE BELONGS TO ORDINARY MEN AND ORDINARY WOMEN, AND THAT FUTURE MUST BE BUILT FREE OF SUCH ACTS AS THESE, MUST BE FOUGHT FOR AND RENEWED LIKE FRESH WATER.
BECAUSE A MESSAGE MUST BE SENT TO THOSE WHO MISTAKE COMPASSION FOR WEAKNESS. A MESSAGE SENT ACROSS SIX THOUSAND YEARS OF RECORDED BLOOD AND STRUGGLE.
AND THE MESSAGE IS THIS:
WHATEVER OUR HISTORY, WHATEVER THE ROOT OF OUR SURNAMES, WE REMAIN A GOOD AND DECENT PEOPLE, AND WE DO NOT BOW DOWN AND WE DO NOT GIVE UP.
THE FIRE OF THE HUMAN SPIRIT CANNOT BE QUENCHED BY BOMB BLASTS OR BODY COUNTS.
CANNOT BE INTIMIDATED FOREVER INTO SILENCE OR DROWNED BY TEARS.
WE HAVE ENDURED WORSE BEFORE; WE WILL BEAR THIS BURDEN AND ALL THAT COME HEREAFTER, BECAUSE THAT'S WHAT ORDINARY MEN AND WOMEN DO.
NO MATTER WHAT.
THIS HAS NOT WEAKENED US.
IT HAS ONLY MADE US STRONGER.

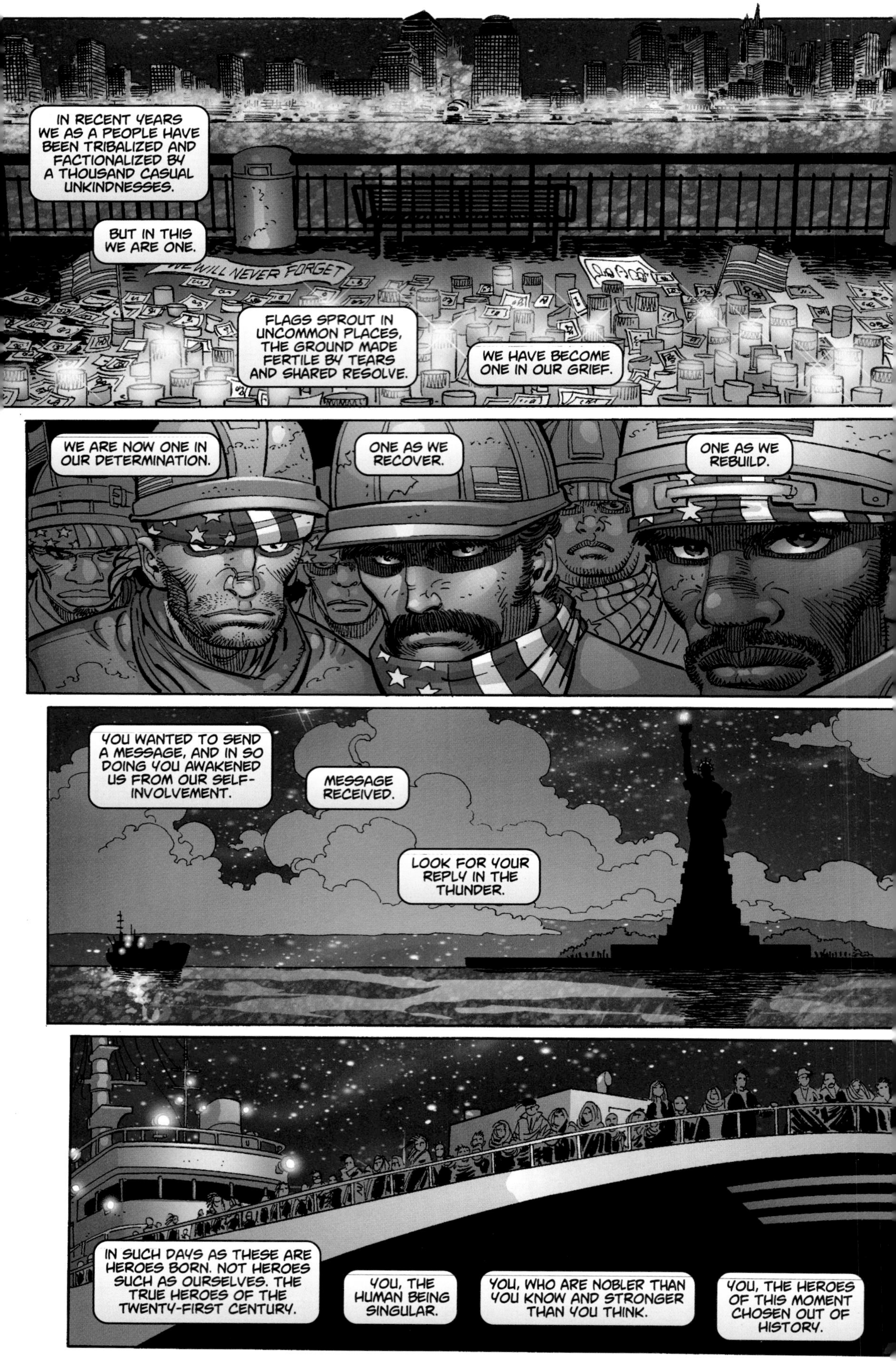
IN RECENT YEARS WE AS A PEOPLE HAVE BEEN TRIBALIZED AND FACTIONALIZED BY A THOUSAND CASUAL UNKINDNESSES.
BUT IN THIS WE ARE ONE.
WE WILL NEVER FORGET
FLAGS SPROUT IN UNCOMMON PLACES, THE GROUND MADE FERTILE BY TEARS AND SHARED RESOLVE.
WE HAVE BECOME ONE IN OUR GRIEF.
WE ARE NOW ONE IN OUR DETERMINATION.
ONE AS WE RECOVER.
ONE AS WE REBUILD.
YOU WANTED TO SEND A MESSAGE, AND IN SO DOING YOU AWAKENED US FROM OUR SELF-INVOLVEMENT.
MESSAGE RECEIVED.
LOOK FOR YOUR REPLY IN THE THUNDER.
IN SUCH DAYS AS THESE ARE HEROES BORN. NOT HEROES SUCH AS OURSELVES. THE TRUE HEROES OF THE TWENTY-FIRST CENTURY.
YOU, THE HUMAN BEING SINGULAR.
YOU, WHO ARE NOBLER THAN YOU KNOW AND STRONGER THAN YOU THINK.
YOU, THE HEROES OF THIS MOMENT CHOSEN OUT OF HISTORY.

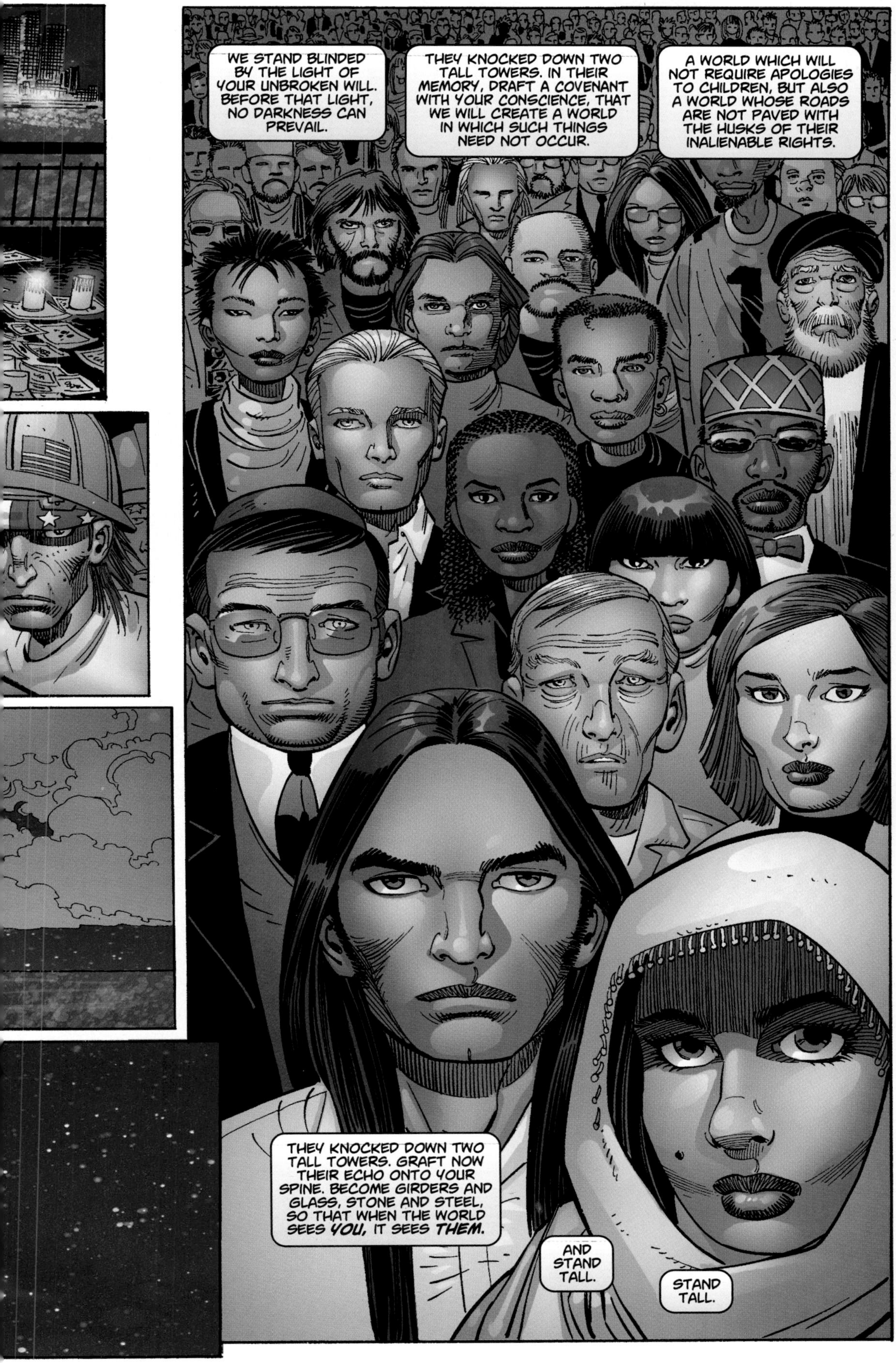
WE STAND BLINDED BY THE LIGHT OF YOUR UNBROKEN WILL. BEFORE THAT LIGHT, NO DARKNESS CAN PREVAIL.
THEY KNOCKED DOWN TWO TALL TOWERS. IN THEIR MEMORY, DRAFT A COVENANT WITH YOUR CONSCIENCE, THAT WE WILL CREATE A WORLD IN WHICH SUCH THINGS NEED NOT OCCUR.
A WORLD WHICH WILL NOT REQUIRE APOLOGIES TO CHILDREN, BUT ALSO A WORLD WHOSE ROADS ARE NOT PAVED WITH THE HUSKS OF THEIR INALIENABLE RIGHTS.
THEY KNOCKED DOWN TWO TALL TOWERS. GRAFT NOW THEIR ECHO ONTO YOUR SPINE. BECOME GIRDERS AND GLASS, STONE AND STEEL, SO THAT WHEN THE WORLD SEES *YOU*, IT SEES *THEM*.
AND STAND TALL.
STAND TALL.

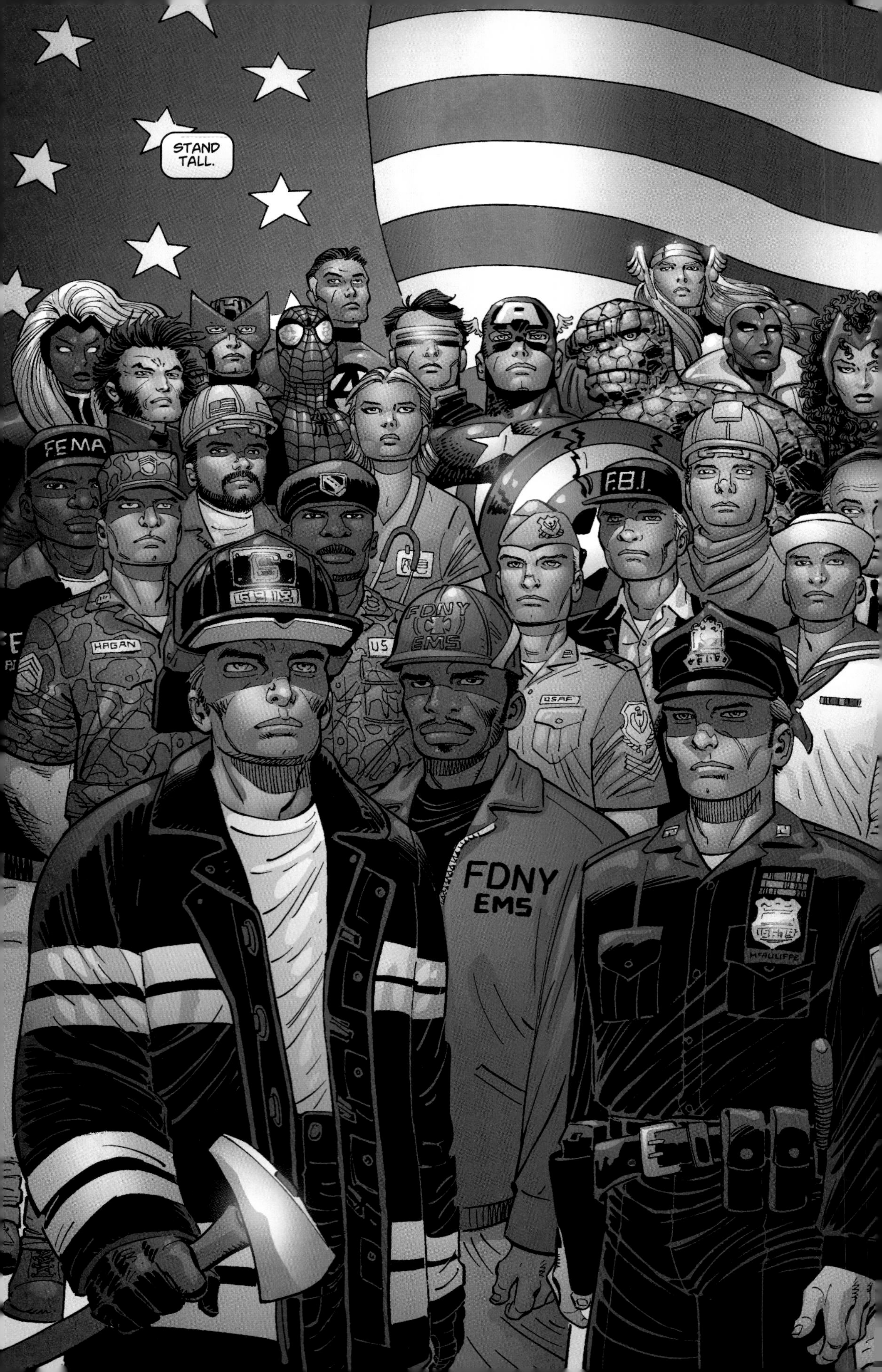
STAND TALL.
FEMA
HAGAN
FDNY EMS
US
F.B.I.
USAF
FDNY EMS
McAULIFFE

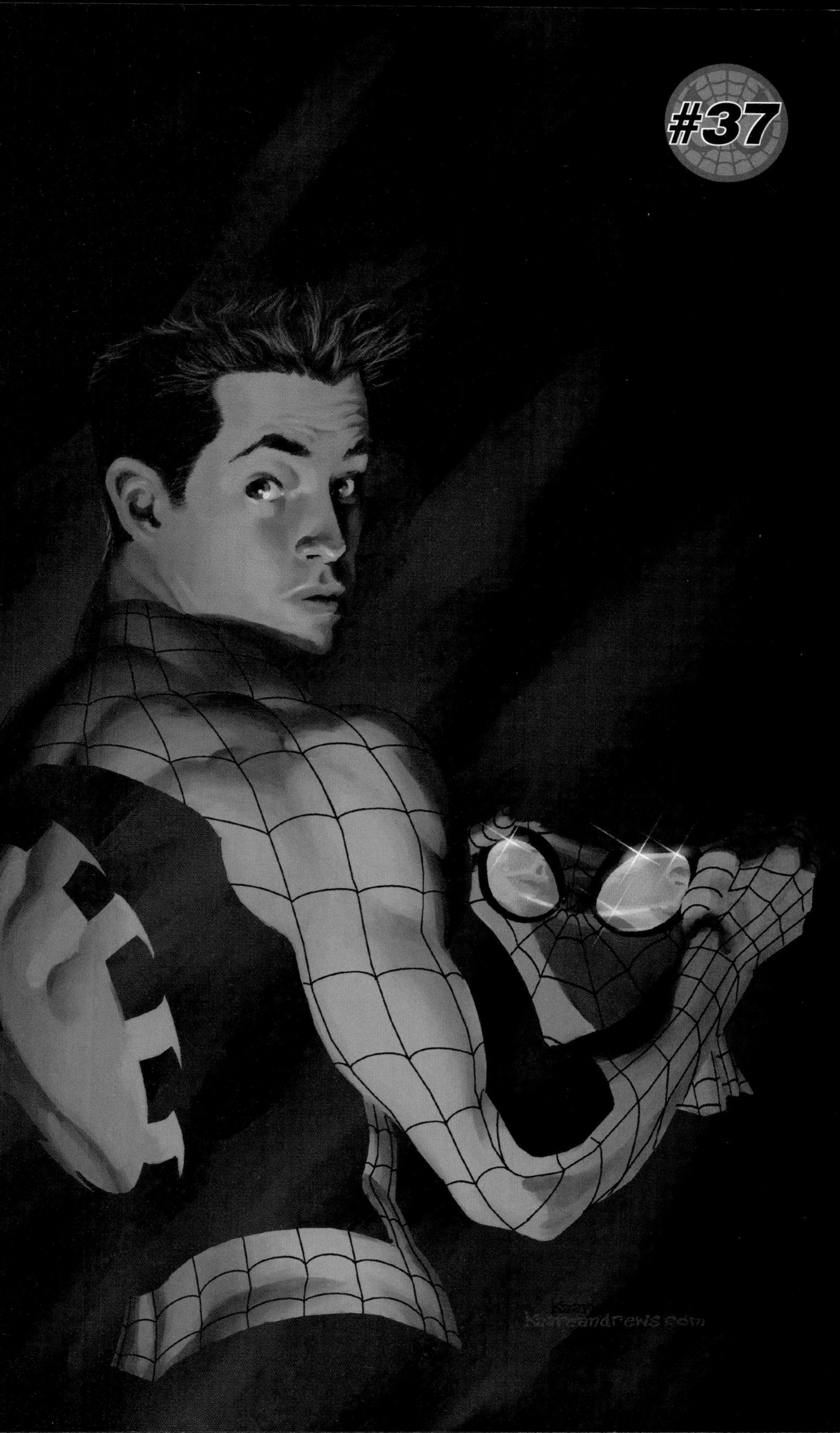
#37
kaareandrews.com

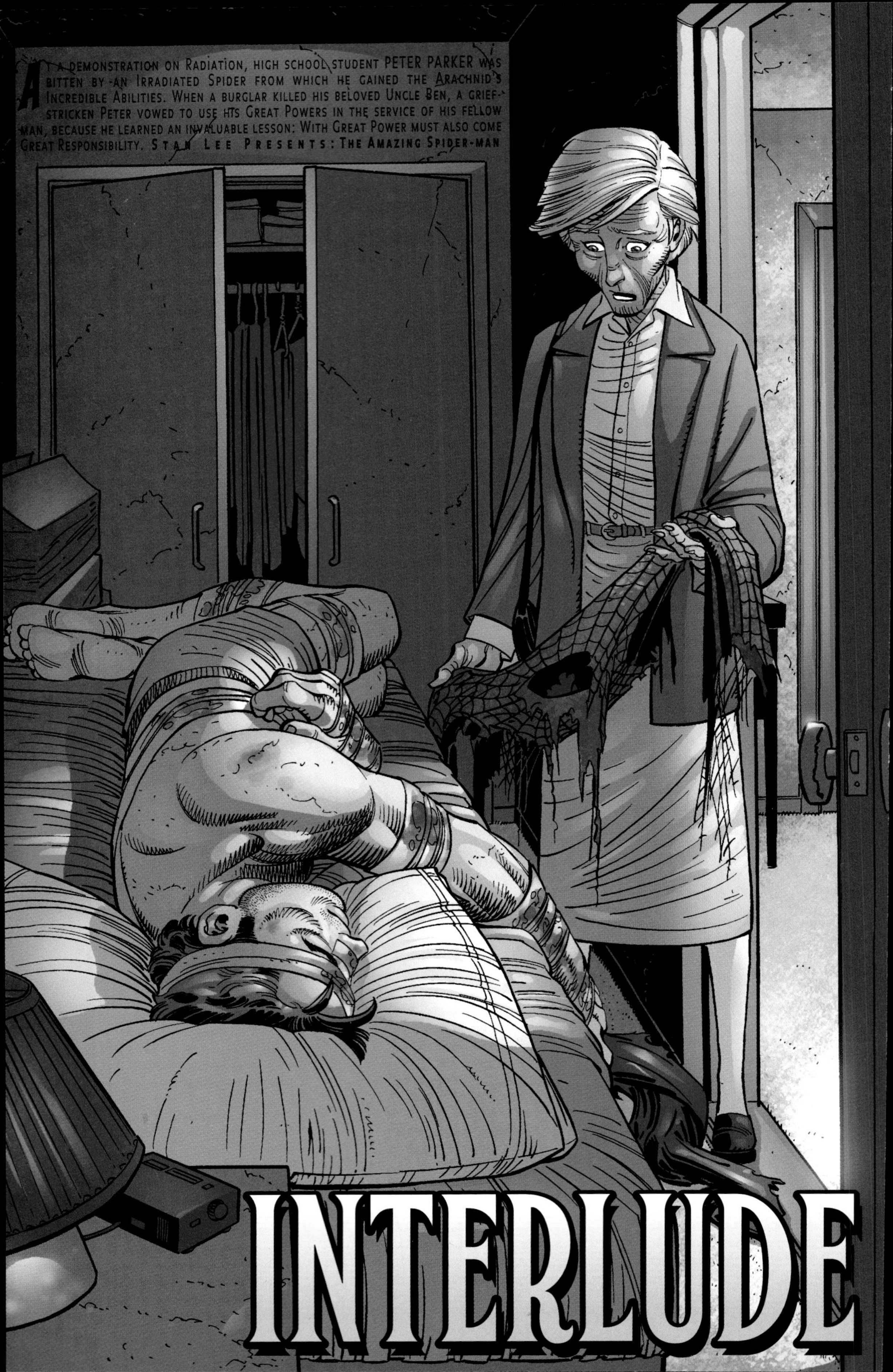
At a demonstration on Radiation, high school student PETER PARKER was bitten by an Irradiated Spider from which he gained the Arachnid's Incredible Abilities. When a burglar killed his beloved Uncle Ben, a grief-stricken Peter vowed to use his Great Powers in the service of his fellow man, because he learned an invaluable lesson: With Great Power must also come Great Responsibility. Stan Lee Presents: The Amazing Spider-Man
INTERLUDE

I ♥ NY

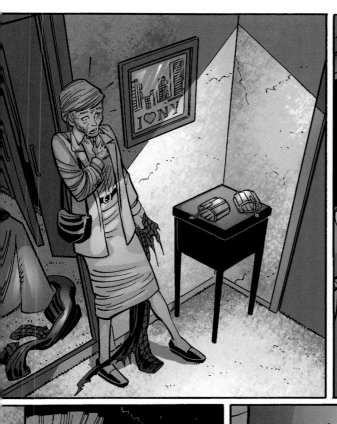

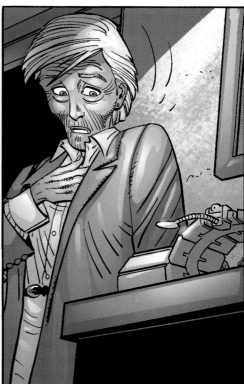

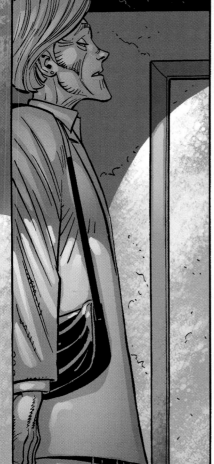

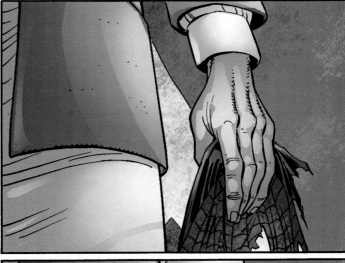

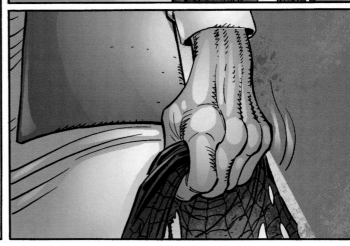

...SNORF... HURMF...

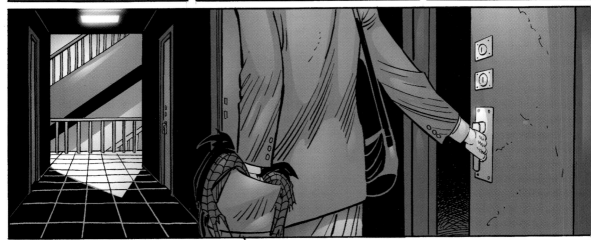

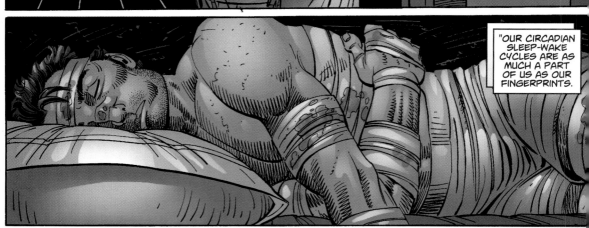

"OUR CIRCADIAN SLEEP-WAKE CYCLES ARE AS MUCH A PART OF US AS OUR FINGERPRINTS.

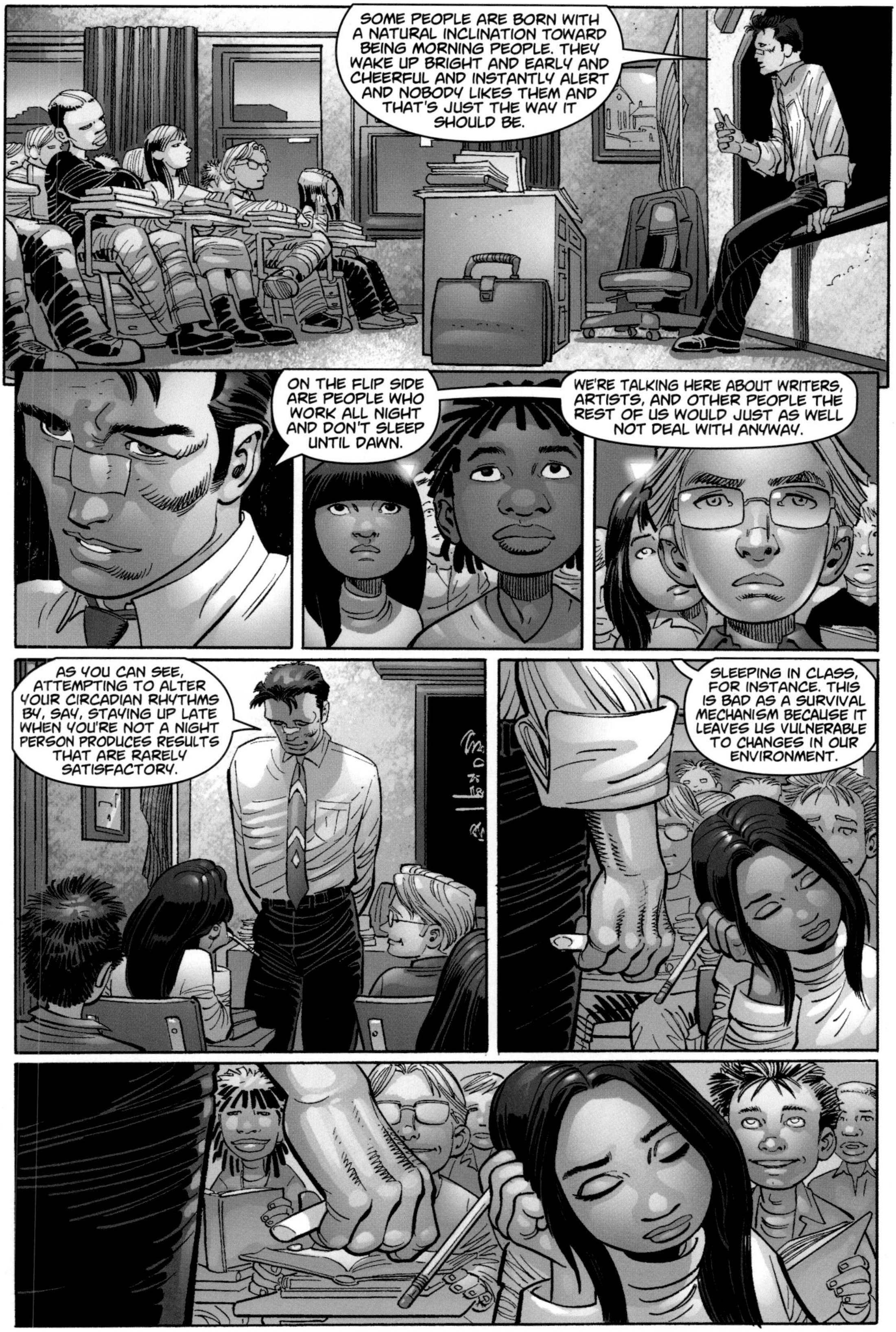
SOME PEOPLE ARE BORN WITH A NATURAL INCLINATION TOWARD BEING MORNING PEOPLE. THEY WAKE UP BRIGHT AND EARLY AND CHEERFUL AND INSTANTLY ALERT AND NOBODY LIKES THEM AND THAT'S JUST THE WAY IT SHOULD BE.
ON THE FLIP SIDE ARE PEOPLE WHO WORK ALL NIGHT AND DON'T SLEEP UNTIL DAWN.
WE'RE TALKING HERE ABOUT WRITERS, ARTISTS, AND OTHER PEOPLE THE REST OF US WOULD JUST AS WELL NOT DEAL WITH ANYWAY.
AS YOU CAN SEE, ATTEMPTING TO ALTER YOUR CIRCADIAN RHYTHMS BY, SAY, STAYING UP LATE WHEN YOU'RE NOT A NIGHT PERSON PRODUCES RESULTS THAT ARE RARELY SATISFACTORY.
SLEEPING IN CLASS, FOR INSTANCE. THIS IS BAD AS A SURVIVAL MECHANISM BECAUSE IT LEAVES US VULNERABLE TO CHANGES IN OUR ENVIRONMENT.

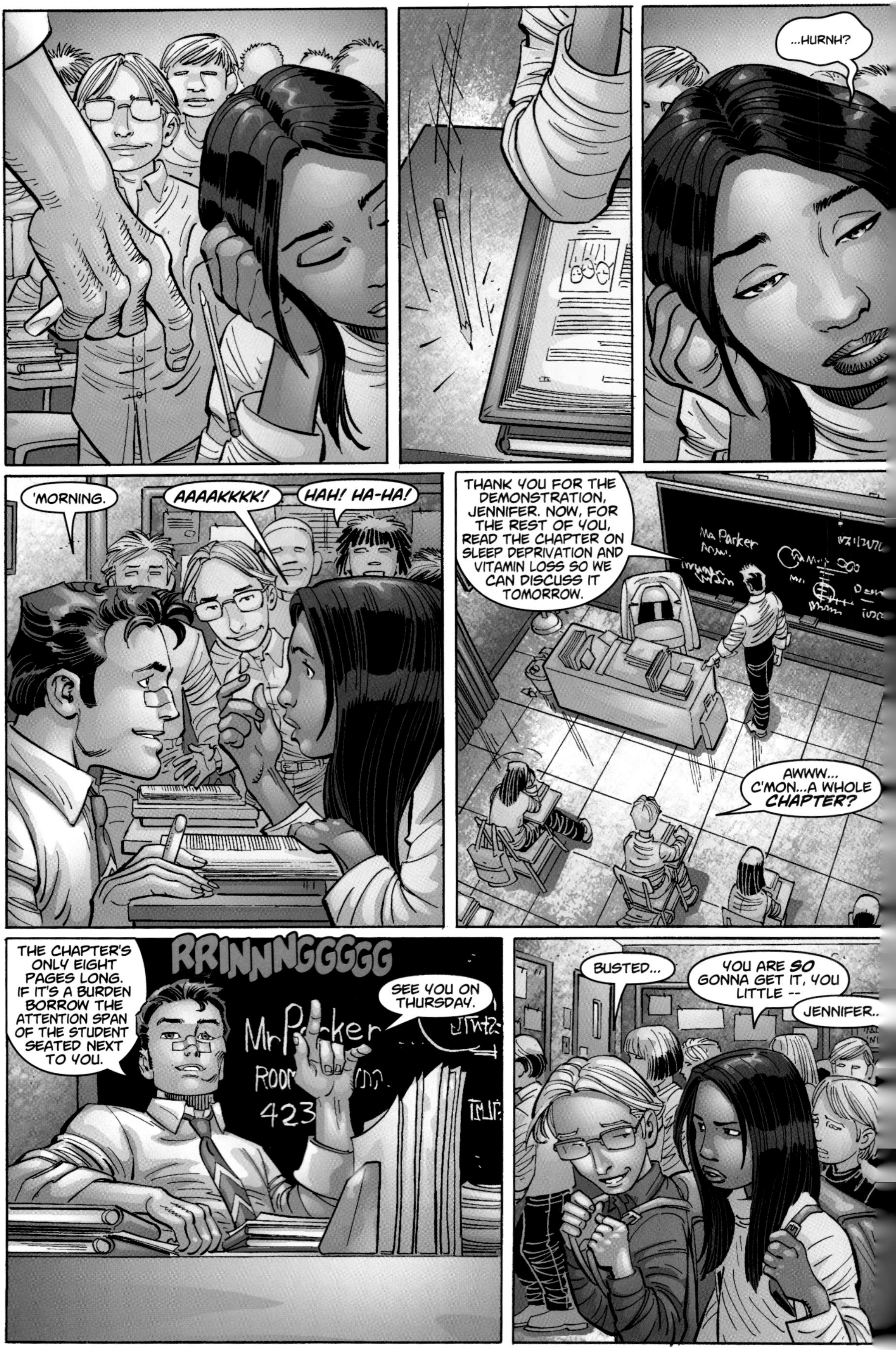
...HURNH?
'MORNING.
AAAAKKKK!
HAH! HA-HA!
THANK YOU FOR THE DEMONSTRATION, JENNIFER. NOW, FOR THE REST OF YOU, READ THE CHAPTER ON SLEEP DEPRIVATION AND VITAMIN LOSS SO WE CAN DISCUSS IT TOMORROW.
Mr Parker
AWWW... C'MON...A WHOLE CHAPTER?
THE CHAPTER'S ONLY EIGHT PAGES LONG. IF IT'S A BURDEN BORROW THE ATTENTION SPAN OF THE STUDENT SEATED NEXT TO YOU.
RRINNNGGGGG
SEE YOU ON THURSDAY.
Mr Parker
423
BUSTED...
YOU ARE SO GONNA GET IT, YOU LITTLE --
JENNIFER..

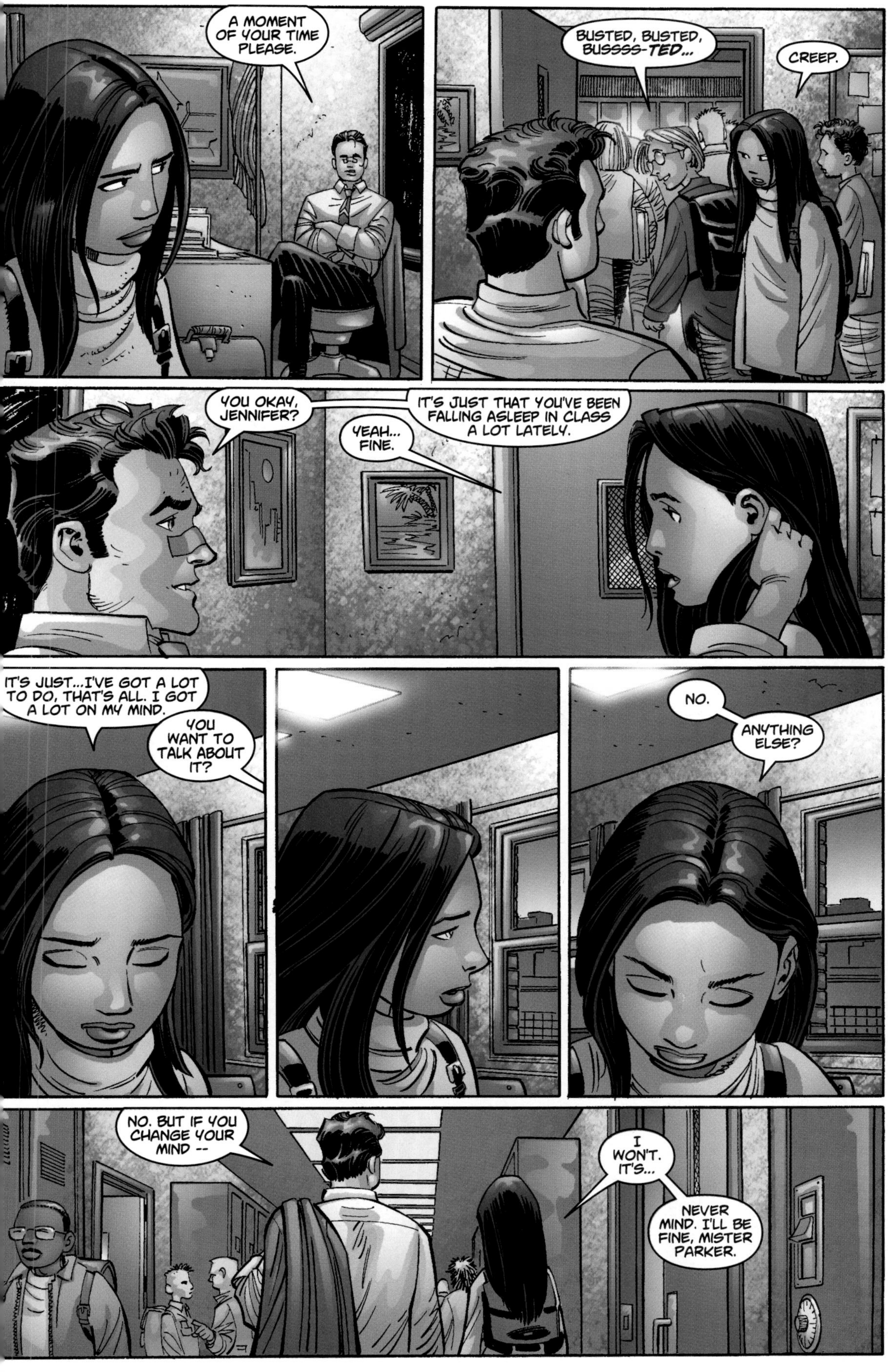
A MOMENT OF YOUR TIME PLEASE.
BUSTED, BUSTED, BUSSSS-*TED*...
CREEP.
YOU OKAY, JENNIFER?
IT'S JUST THAT YOU'VE BEEN FALLING ASLEEP IN CLASS A LOT LATELY.
YEAH... FINE.
IT'S JUST...I'VE GOT A LOT TO DO, THAT'S ALL. I GOT A LOT ON MY MIND.
YOU WANT TO TALK ABOUT IT?
NO.
ANYTHING ELSE?
NO. BUT IF YOU CHANGE YOUR MIND --
I WON'T. IT'S...
NEVER MIND. I'LL BE FINE, MISTER PARKER.

PETER.

DOMINIC.

HOW'S IT GOING?

OKAY... I GUESS.

AH. JENNIFER...

YEAH, I CAUGHT THE LAST PART OF THAT. SAD CASE.

SAD HOW?

I HAD HER IN MY CLASS LAST YEAR. TROUBLED KID. I FIGURED IT WAS DRUGS. CLOSE, BUT NOT CORRECT. SHE'S CLEAN, AS FAR AS I KNOW.

"SO WHAT'S THE PROBLEM THEN? I MEAN, YOU SAID SHE WAS A SAD CASE."

"SHE IS. BUT NOT FOR THE USUAL REASONS."

"HER BROTHER'S A USER. HE'S BEEN SUSPENDED TWICE IN THE LAST YEAR FOR BEING HIGH. HE GETS HER TO DO HIS HOMEWORK, HELP HIM TAKE CARE OF THINGS, COVER FOR HIM."

"SHAME, REALLY."

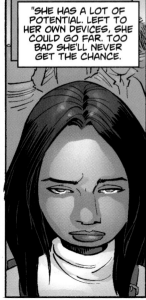

"SHE HAS A LOT OF POTENTIAL. LEFT TO HER OWN DEVICES, SHE COULD GO FAR. TOO BAD SHE'LL NEVER GET THE CHANCE.

"THE BAD ONES ALWAYS DRAG THE GOOD ONES DOWN WITH THEM. ALWAYS DO, PETER."

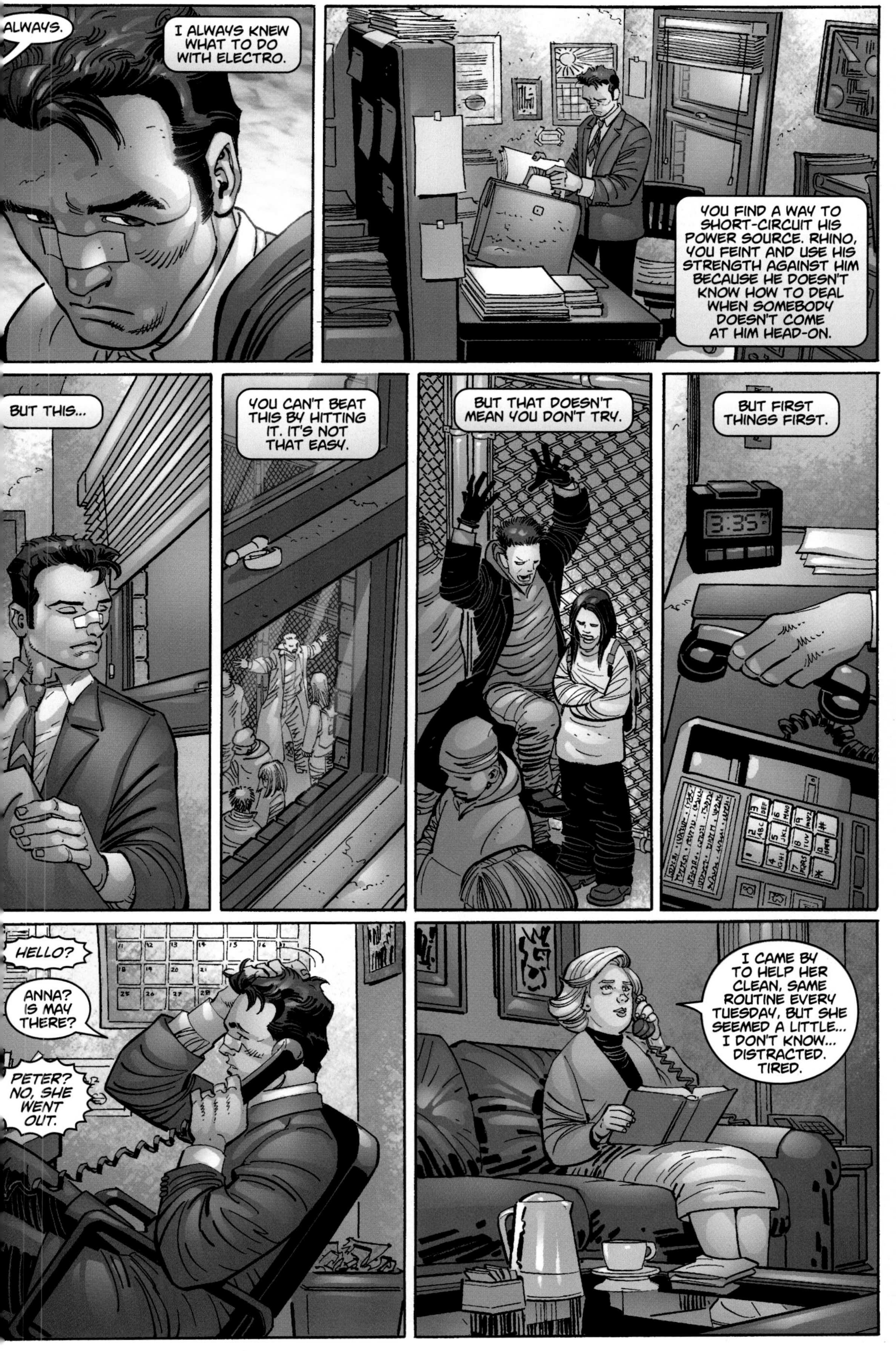
ALWAYS.
I ALWAYS KNEW WHAT TO DO WITH ELECTRO.
YOU FIND A WAY TO SHORT-CIRCUIT HIS POWER SOURCE. RHINO, YOU FEINT AND USE HIS STRENGTH AGAINST HIM BECAUSE HE DOESN'T KNOW HOW TO DEAL WHEN SOMEBODY DOESN'T COME AT HIM HEAD-ON.
BUT THIS...
YOU CAN'T BEAT THIS BY HITTING IT. IT'S NOT THAT EASY.
BUT THAT DOESN'T MEAN YOU DON'T TRY.
BUT FIRST THINGS FIRST.
3:35
HELLO?
ANNA? IS MAY THERE?
PETER? NO, SHE WENT OUT.
I CAME BY TO HELP HER CLEAN, SAME ROUTINE EVERY TUESDAY, BUT SHE SEEMED A LITTLE... I DON'T KNOW... DISTRACTED. TIRED.

EASTSIDE COMMUNITY ☆☆☆☆ PLAYHOUSE

WHY, IS THERE A PROBLEM?

NO...NO PROBLEM, IT'S JUST...WELL, I ALWAYS TRY TO CALL HER THIS TIME OF DAY, AND SHE'S ALWAYS THERE.

"EVERYTHING CHANGES, PETER. YOU CAN'T EXPECT PEOPLE TO STAY FROZEN IN TIME FOREVER, YOU KNOW."

"YEAH...YEAH, I GUESS SO.

"WELL, IF YOU SEE HER FIRST, SAY HI FOR ME AND TELL HER I LOVE HER."

"I WILL, PETER. 'BYE.

HMMM...

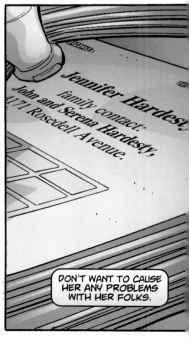

Jennifer Hardesty

family contact: John and Serena Hardesty, 4171 Rosedell Avenue.

DON'T WANT TO CAUSE HER ANY PROBLEMS WITH HER FOLKS.

217TH N

BUT IT PROBABLY WOULDN'T HURT TO WALK HOME A DIFFERENT WAY TODAY.

JUST FOR THE VARIETY.

SPARE SOME CHANGE, MISTER?

CAN I GET A QUARTER FOR FOOD?

CAN WE HAVE SOME MONEY FOR POT? C'MON, AT LEAST WE'RE HONEST ABOUT IT...

HUH...

NYC COND CONDEMNED N

4 1 7 1

ADDRESS MATCHES. BUT FROM THE LOOK OF THE PLACE NOBODY'S LIVED HERE FOR AT LEAST A YEAR.

EXCUSE ME, MA'AM --

I'M NOT A MA'AM, I'M A MISSUS.

I DIDN'T --

MA'AM MEANS MADAM, AND I AIN'T FRENCH AND I AIN'T RUNNING AN ESCORT SERVICE HERE, UNLIKE CERTAIN *OTHER* PEOPLE I COULD NAME ACROSS THE STREET, I DON'T LIKE TO TALK, BUT THERE IT IS --

I JUST WANT TO KNOW --

-- I'M A *MISSUS* WHICH IS *MRS.* WHICH IS *MARRIED* AND I'M *PROUD* OF IT I DON'T CARE *WHAT* MY SISTER SAYS SHE DOESN'T KNOW WHAT I HAVE TO DEAL WITH EVERY DAY, THE NOISE, THE PEOPLE --

HEY!

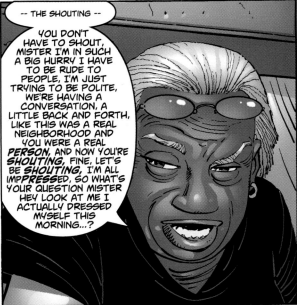

-- THE SHOUTING --

YOU DON'T HAVE TO SHOUT, MISTER I'M IN SUCH A BIG HURRY I HAVE TO BE RUDE TO PEOPLE, I'M JUST TRYING TO BE POLITE, WE'RE HAVING A CONVERSATION, A LITTLE BACK AND FORTH, LIKE THIS WAS A REAL NEIGHBORHOOD AND YOU WERE A REAL *PERSON,* AND NOW YOU'RE *SHOUTING,* FINE, LET'S BE *SHOUTING,* I'M ALL IMP*PRESSED,* SO WHAT'S YOUR QUESTION MISTER HEY LOOK AT ME I ACTUALLY DRESSED MYSELF THIS MORNING...?

I CAN BENCH PRESS MORE THAN ANY TWO MEMBERS OF THE X-MEN.

I CAN TEAR THROUGH A CONCRETE WALL WITH ONE HAND.

I'M REASONABLY SURE I CAN TAKE HER.

WHAT.

HAPPENED.

TO.

4171.

ROSEDELL.

OH, *THAT*. YOU WANT TO KNOW ABOUT *THAT*. IT'S CONDEMNED. YOU SEE THAT SIGN, THE ONE WITH THE WORD *CONDEMNED* ON IT?

USED TO BE A FAMILY LIVING THERE. DAD WAS A CREEP, RAN OUT. THE MOTHER WASN'T MUCH BETTER. TOOK OFF ABOUT THE SAME TIME AS THE BUILDING WAS CONDEMNED. NOT VERY NICE PEOPLE.

RUDE.

LIKED TO SHOUT A LOT. BUT YOU WOULDN'T KNOW ANYTHING ABOUT THAT, WOULD YOU?

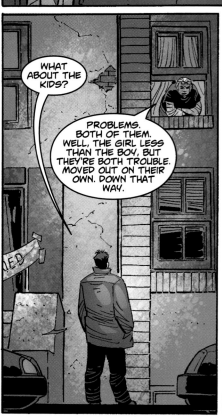

WHAT ABOUT THE KIDS?

PROBLEMS. BOTH OF THEM. WELL, THE GIRL LESS THAN THE BOY, BUT THEY'RE BOTH TROUBLE. MOVED OUT ON THEIR OWN. DOWN THAT WAY.

THEY LIVE IN THERE?

YEAH. I SUPPOSE. IF YOU CAN CALL THAT LIVING. IT WON'T END WELL, YOU KNOW. NEVER DOES.

THANKS.

SURE, KNOCK YOURSELF OUT.

EXCUSE ME, MA'AM --

IT'S NOT *MA'AM*, IT'S *MISSUS*...

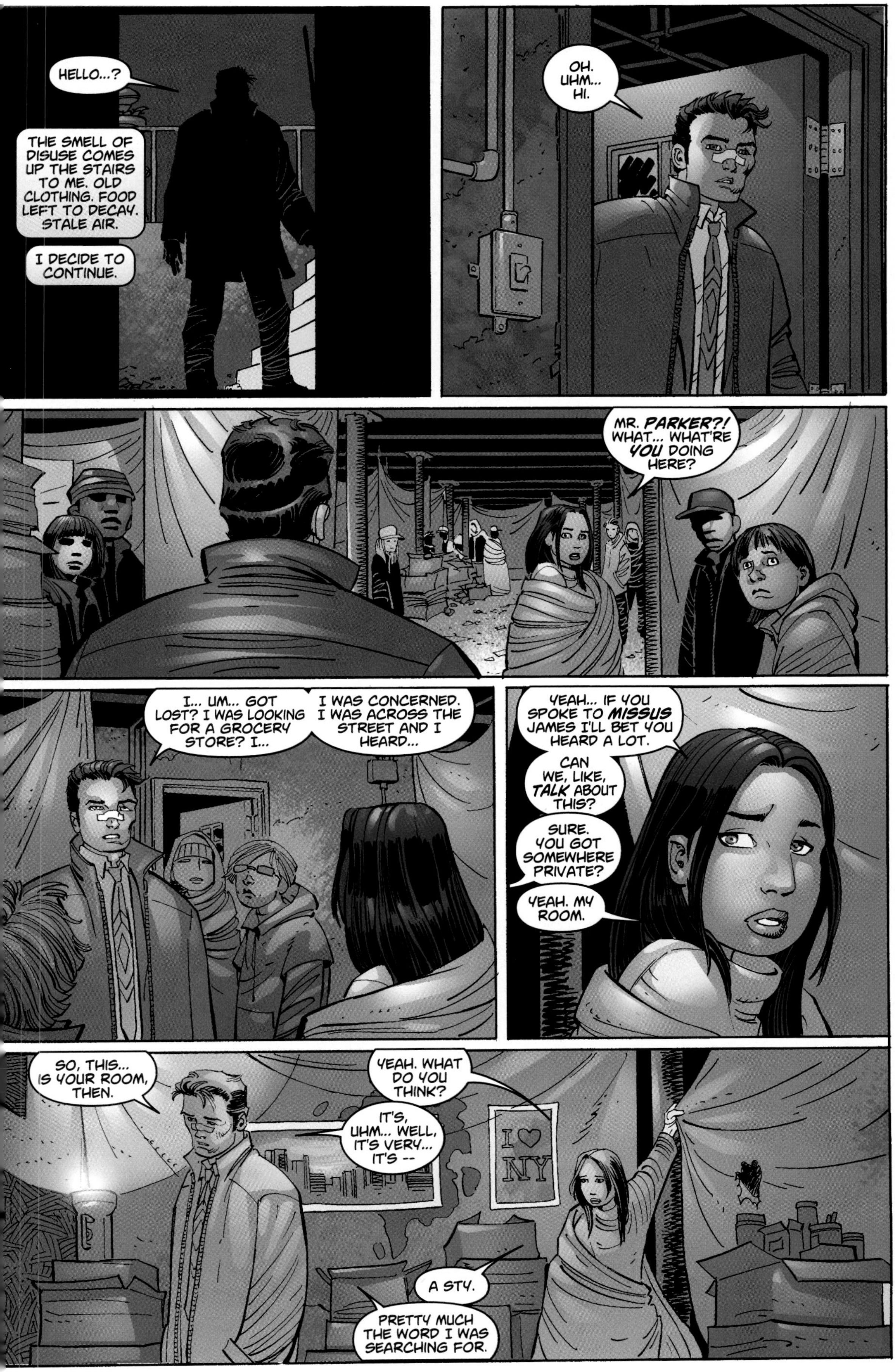
HELLO...?
THE SMELL OF DISUSE COMES UP THE STAIRS TO ME. OLD CLOTHING. FOOD LEFT TO DECAY. STALE AIR.
I DECIDE TO CONTINUE.
OH. UHM... HI.
MR. PARKER?! WHAT... WHAT'RE YOU DOING HERE?
I... UM... GOT LOST? I WAS LOOKING FOR A GROCERY STORE? I...
I WAS CONCERNED. I WAS ACROSS THE STREET AND I HEARD...
YEAH... IF YOU SPOKE TO MISSUS JAMES I'LL BET YOU HEARD A LOT.
CAN WE, LIKE, TALK ABOUT THIS?
SURE. YOU GOT SOMEWHERE PRIVATE?
YEAH. MY ROOM.
SO, THIS... IS YOUR ROOM, THEN.
YEAH. WHAT DO YOU THINK?
IT'S, UHM... WELL, IT'S VERY... IT'S --
A STY.
PRETTY MUCH THE WORD I WAS SEARCHING FOR.

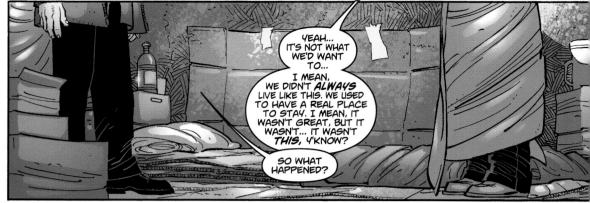

YEAH... IT'S NOT WHAT WE'D WANT TO... I MEAN, WE DIDN'T *ALWAYS* LIVE LIKE THIS. WE USED TO HAVE A REAL PLACE TO STAY. I MEAN, IT WASN'T GREAT, BUT IT WASN'T... IT WASN'T *THIS*, Y'KNOW?

SO WHAT HAPPENED?

SAME THING AS HAPPENED TO THE OTHER KIDS OUT THERE. WE GOT KICKED OUT. WHAT, YOU THINK EVERY KID IN THE STREET RAN AWAY, OR IS ON DRUGS OR STUFF? WE GOT THE BOOT, MR. PARKER.

WE WENT TO LIVE WITH OUR AUNT FOR A WHILE, BUT SHE DIDN'T WANT US ANY MORE THAN THEY DID. YOU KNOW WHAT IT'S LIKE, TO HAVE TO GO FIND RELATIVES TO LIVE WITH BECAUSE YOUR FOLKS AREN'T AROUND ANYMORE?

YOU MAY NOT BELIEVE IT, BUT YEAH...

"...I DO. I LOST MY FOLKS WHEN I WAS A KID.

"SHE GOT ME THROUGH... WELL, EVERYTHING, I GUESS. TOOK CARE OF ME, RAISED ME LIKE HER OWN."

"DOES SHE LOVE YOU?"

"YEAH... SHE DOES."

"THEN YOU'RE LUCKY."

"I GUESS I AM."

WE WEREN'T. FINALLY, STEVE AND I JUST HAD TO GET OUT.

STEVE'S YOUR BROTHER?

YEAH. I KINDA LOOK AFTER HIM. HELP HIM WITH HIS HOMEWORK AND STUFF.

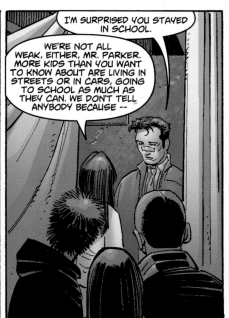

I'M SURPRISED YOU STAYED IN SCHOOL.

WE'RE NOT ALL WEAK, EITHER, MR. PARKER. MORE KIDS THAN YOU WANT TO KNOW ABOUT ARE LIVING IN STREETS OR IN CARS, GOING TO SCHOOL AS MUCH AS THEY CAN. WE DON'T TELL ANYBODY BECAUSE --

WELL, WE JUST CAN'T, THAT'S ALL. THEY'D KICK US OUT, OR WE'D HAVE TO GO TO A FOSTER HOME, AND THE OTHER KIDS...IT'S BETTER THIS WAY.

WE HIT THE STREETS A LOT, ASKING FOR CHANGE AND STUFF. WE GET A FEW BUCKS HERE AND THERE. IT'S NOT SO BAD. WE CAN EVEN EAT AT McDONALD'S ONCE IN A WHILE.

IT'S JUST... IT'S JUST THE WAY THINGS ARE, Y'KNOW?

THERE'S SUCH PAIN IN HER VOICE. BUT ALSO SUCH STRENGTH.

I PASS BY THIS NEIGHBORHOOD A DOZEN TIMES A MONTH. HOW COULD I NOT KNOW THIS WAS HERE? HOW COULD I NOT SEE THIS?

WORST OF ALL... WHEN DID I STOP SEEING THIS?

PLEASE DON'T TELL ON US, MR. PARKER.

I --

PLEASE. THERE'S NOTHING YOU CAN DO UNLESS YOU WANT TO ADOPT ME AND STEVE AND HALF THE KIDS OUT HERE RIGHT NOW. IF YOU TELL ANYBODY, WE'LL END UP IN A FOSTER HOME OR WORSE.

WE'RE SIX MONTHS FROM GRADUATING, SIX MONTHS FROM BEING LEGAL. CAN YOU GIVE US THAT, MR. PARKER? WE'VE COME THIS FAR ON OUR OWN. WE CAN MAKE IT THE REST OF THE WAY. JUST...LET US.

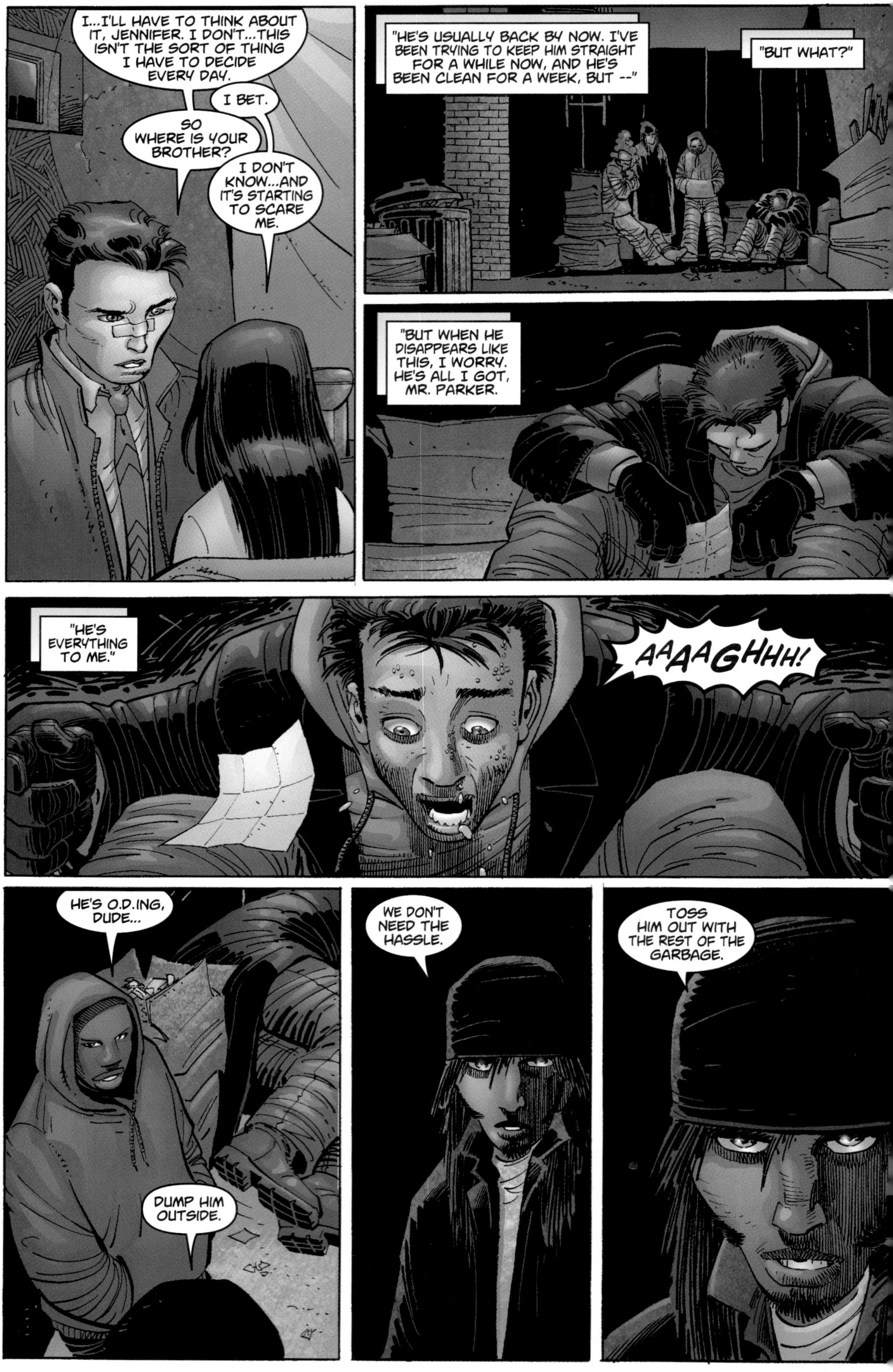
I...I'LL HAVE TO THINK ABOUT IT, JENNIFER. I DON'T...THIS ISN'T THE SORT OF THING I HAVE TO DECIDE EVERY DAY.
I BET.
SO WHERE IS YOUR BROTHER?
I DON'T KNOW...AND IT'S STARTING TO SCARE ME.
"HE'S USUALLY BACK BY NOW. I'VE BEEN TRYING TO KEEP HIM STRAIGHT FOR A WHILE NOW, AND HE'S BEEN CLEAN FOR A WEEK, BUT --"
"BUT WHAT?"
"BUT WHEN HE DISAPPEARS LIKE THIS, I WORRY. HE'S ALL I GOT, MR. PARKER.
"HE'S EVERYTHING TO ME."
AAAAGHHH!
HE'S O.D.ING, DUDE...
DUMP HIM OUTSIDE.
WE DON'T NEED THE HASSLE.
TOSS HIM OUT WITH THE REST OF THE GARBAGE.

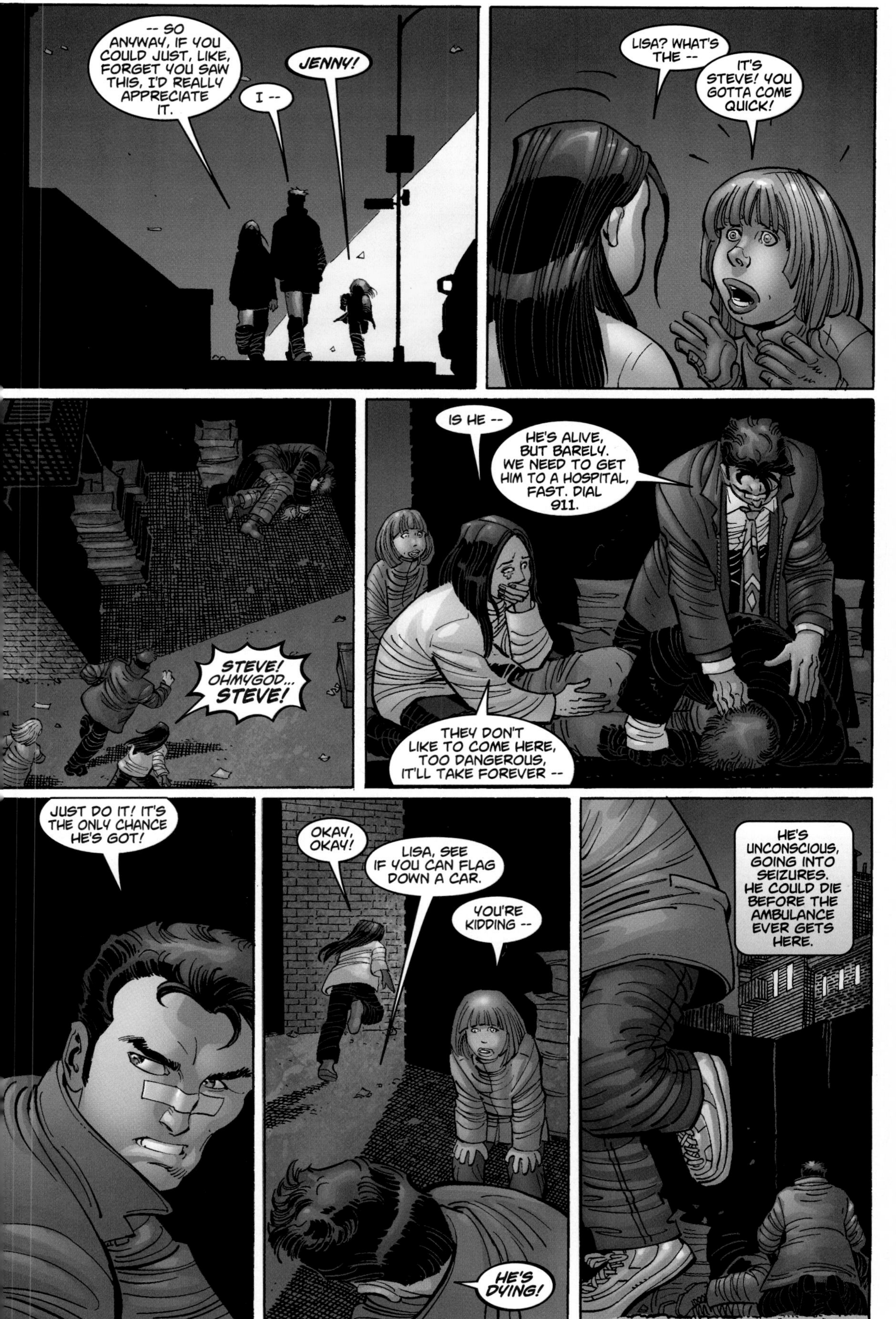
-- SO ANYWAY, IF YOU COULD JUST, LIKE, FORGET YOU SAW THIS, I'D REALLY APPRECIATE IT.
I --
JENNY!
LISA? WHAT'S THE --
IT'S STEVE! YOU GOTTA COME QUICK!
STEVE! OHMYGOD... STEVE!
IS HE --
HE'S ALIVE, BUT BARELY. WE NEED TO GET HIM TO A HOSPITAL, FAST. DIAL 911.
THEY DON'T LIKE TO COME HERE, TOO DANGEROUS, IT'LL TAKE FOREVER --
JUST DO IT! IT'S THE ONLY CHANCE HE'S GOT!
OKAY, OKAY!
LISA, SEE IF YOU CAN FLAG DOWN A CAR.
YOU'RE KIDDING --
HE'S DYING!
HE'S UNCONSCIOUS, GOING INTO SEIZURES. HE COULD DIE BEFORE THE AMBULANCE EVER GETS HERE.

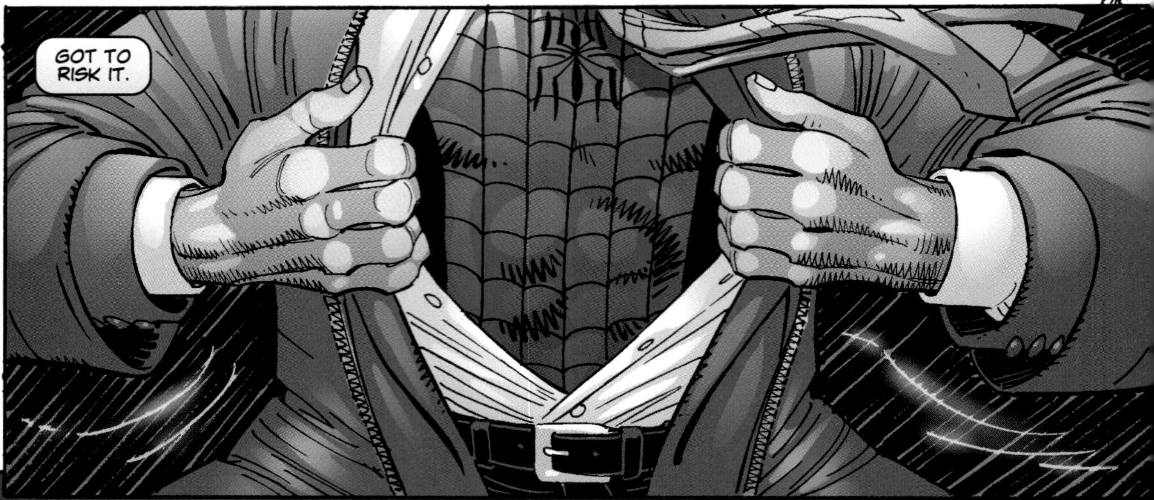
GOT TO RISK IT.

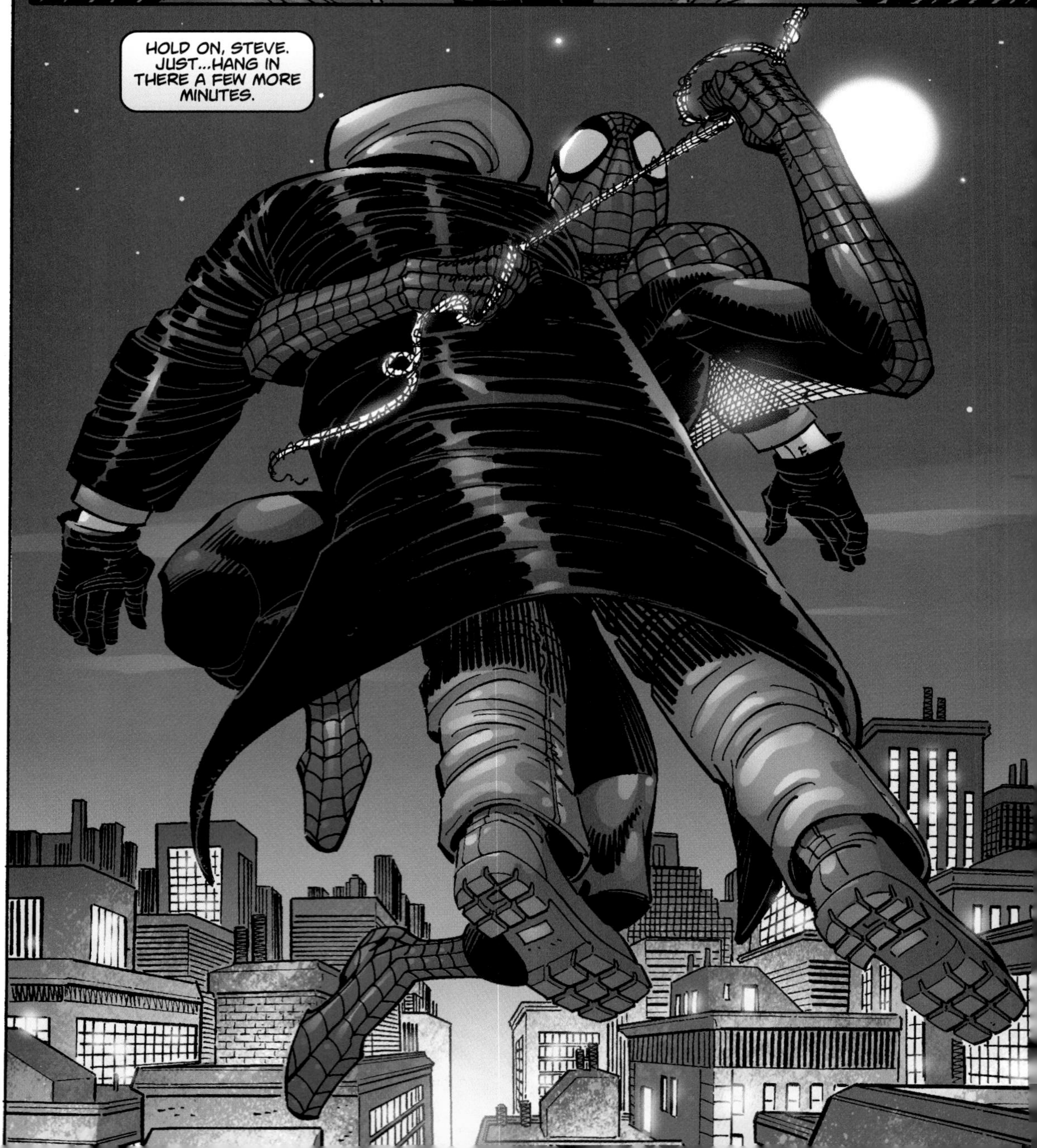
HOLD ON, STEVE. JUST...HANG IN THERE A FEW MORE MINUTES.

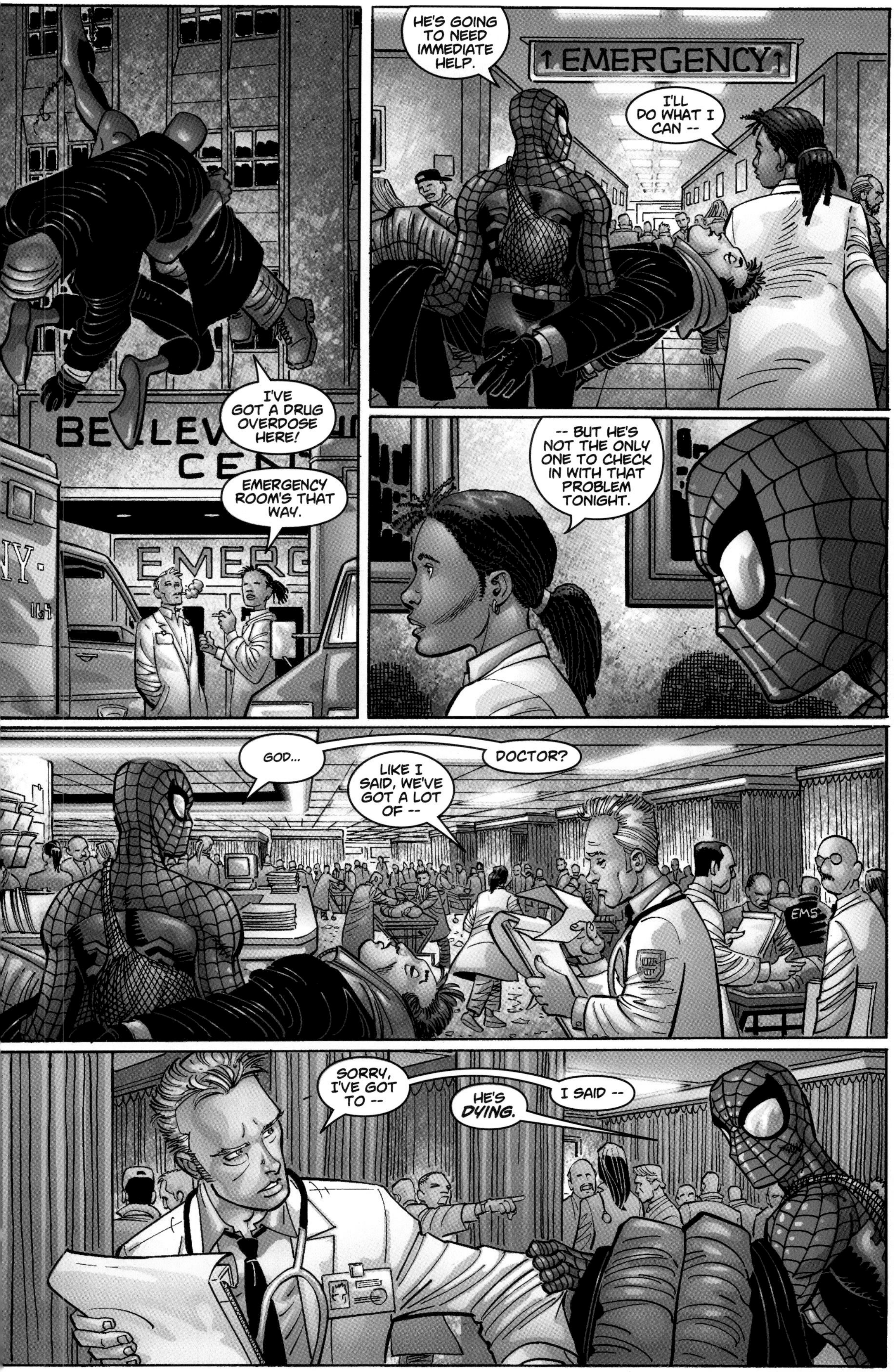

I'VE GOT A DRUG OVERDOSE HERE!
EMERGENCY ROOM'S THAT WAY.
EMERGENCY
HE'S GOING TO NEED IMMEDIATE HELP.
I'LL DO WHAT I CAN --
-- BUT HE'S NOT THE ONLY ONE TO CHECK IN WITH THAT PROBLEM TONIGHT.
GOD...
DOCTOR?
LIKE I SAID, WE'VE GOT A LOT OF --
EMS
SORRY, I'VE GOT TO --
I SAID --
HE'S *DYING.*

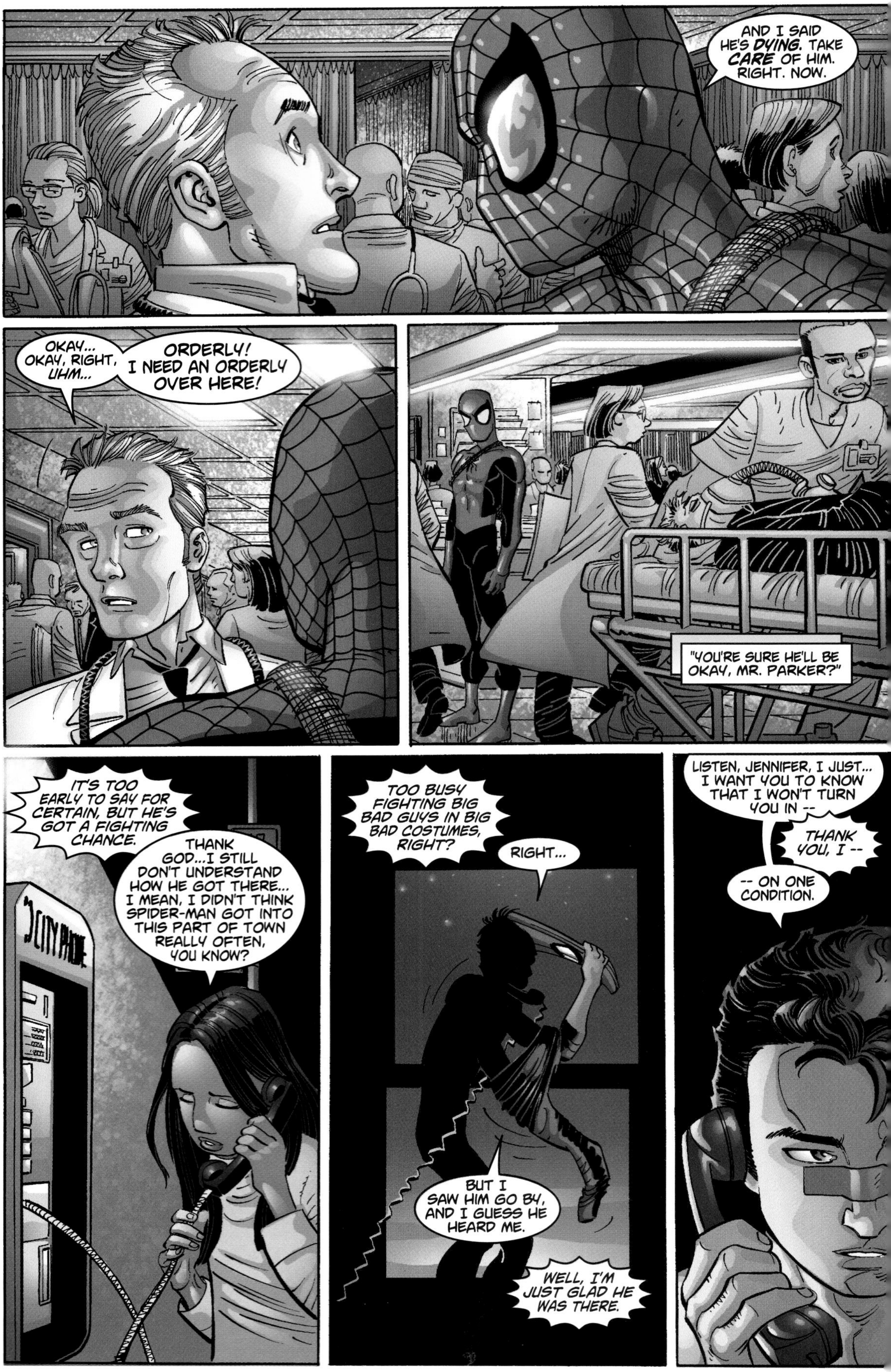
AND I SAID HE'S DYING. TAKE CARE OF HIM. RIGHT. NOW.
OKAY... OKAY, RIGHT, UHM...
ORDERLY! I NEED AN ORDERLY OVER HERE!
"YOU'RE SURE HE'LL BE OKAY, MR. PARKER?"
IT'S TOO EARLY TO SAY FOR CERTAIN, BUT HE'S GOT A FIGHTING CHANCE.
THANK GOD...I STILL DON'T UNDERSTAND HOW HE GOT THERE... I MEAN, I DIDN'T THINK SPIDER-MAN GOT INTO THIS PART OF TOWN REALLY OFTEN, YOU KNOW?
CITY PHONE
TOO BUSY FIGHTING BIG BAD GUYS IN BIG BAD COSTUMES, RIGHT?
RIGHT...
BUT I SAW HIM GO BY, AND I GUESS HE HEARD ME.
WELL, I'M JUST GLAD HE WAS THERE.
LISTEN, JENNIFER, I JUST... I WANT YOU TO KNOW THAT I WON'T TURN YOU IN --
THANK YOU, I --
-- ON ONE CONDITION.

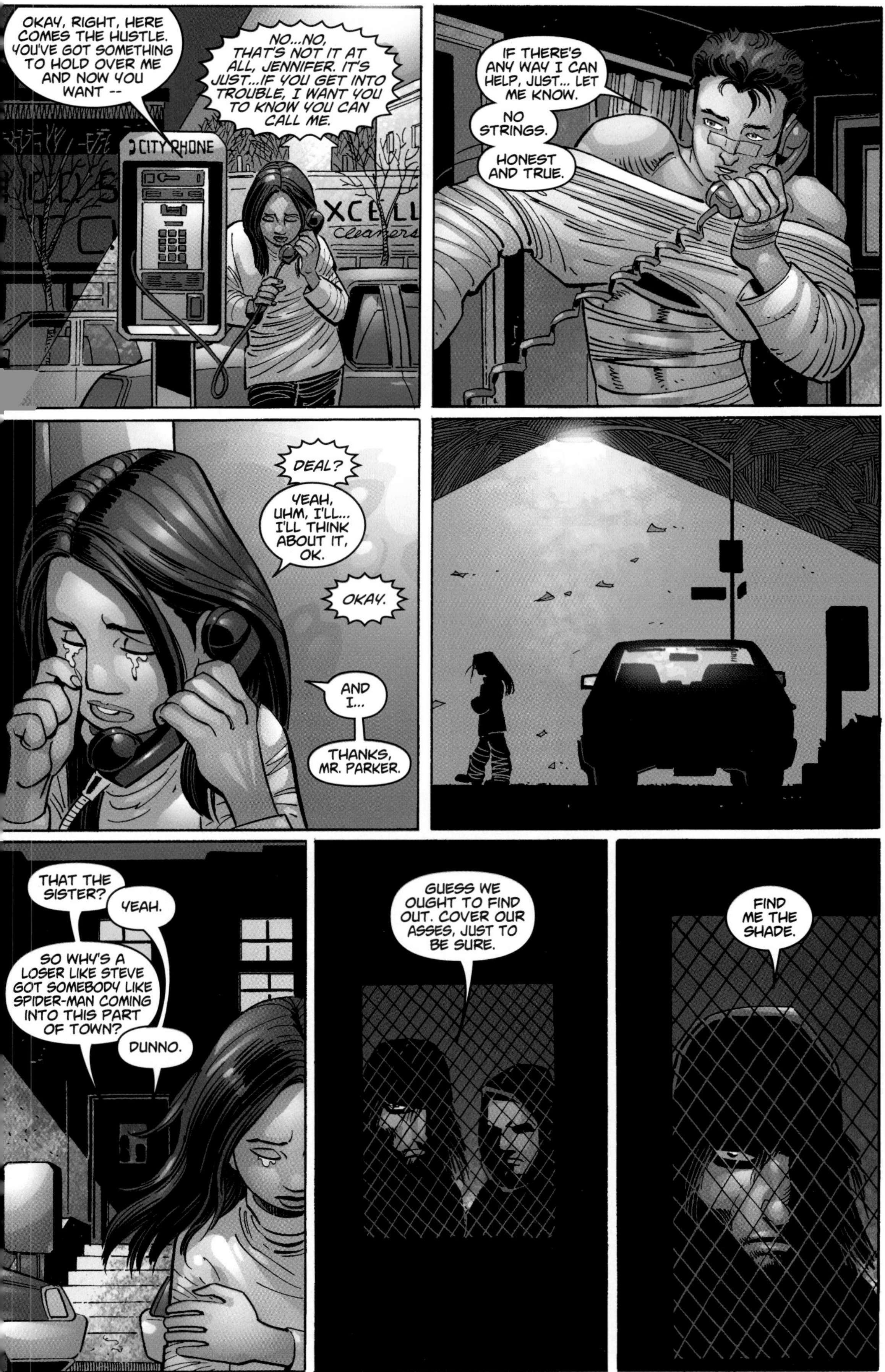

OKAY, RIGHT, HERE COMES THE HUSTLE. YOU'VE GOT SOMETHING TO HOLD OVER ME AND NOW YOU WANT --
NO...NO, THAT'S NOT IT AT ALL, JENNIFER. IT'S JUST...IF YOU GET INTO TROUBLE, I WANT YOU TO KNOW YOU CAN CALL ME.
CITY PHONE
XCELL Cleaners
IF THERE'S ANY WAY I CAN HELP, JUST... LET ME KNOW.
NO STRINGS.
HONEST AND TRUE.
DEAL?
YEAH, UHM, I'LL... I'LL THINK ABOUT IT, OK.
OKAY.
AND I...
THANKS, MR. PARKER.
THAT THE SISTER?
YEAH.
SO WHY'S A LOSER LIKE STEVE GOT SOMEBODY LIKE SPIDER-MAN COMING INTO THIS PART OF TOWN?
DUNNO.
GUESS WE OUGHT TO FIND OUT. COVER OUR ASSES, JUST TO BE SURE.
FIND ME THE SHADE.

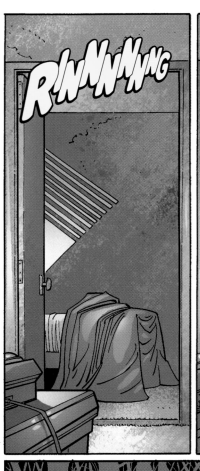

RINNNNNG

JUST A SEC, JUST A SEC, JEEZ...

HULK'S DELI, YOU ORDER, WE SMASH.

...PETER?

AUNT MAY? WELL, IT'S ABOUT TIME YOU SHOWED UP, YOUNG LADY. I WAS STARTING TO GET WORRIED. HOW WAS THE MOVIE?

I...DIDN'T GO TO THE MOVIES, PETER. I'VE BEEN...I'VE BEEN SITTING HERE ALL DAY, JUST...

AUNT MAY? ARE YOU ALL RIGHT?

NO. NO, PETER, I'M NOT.

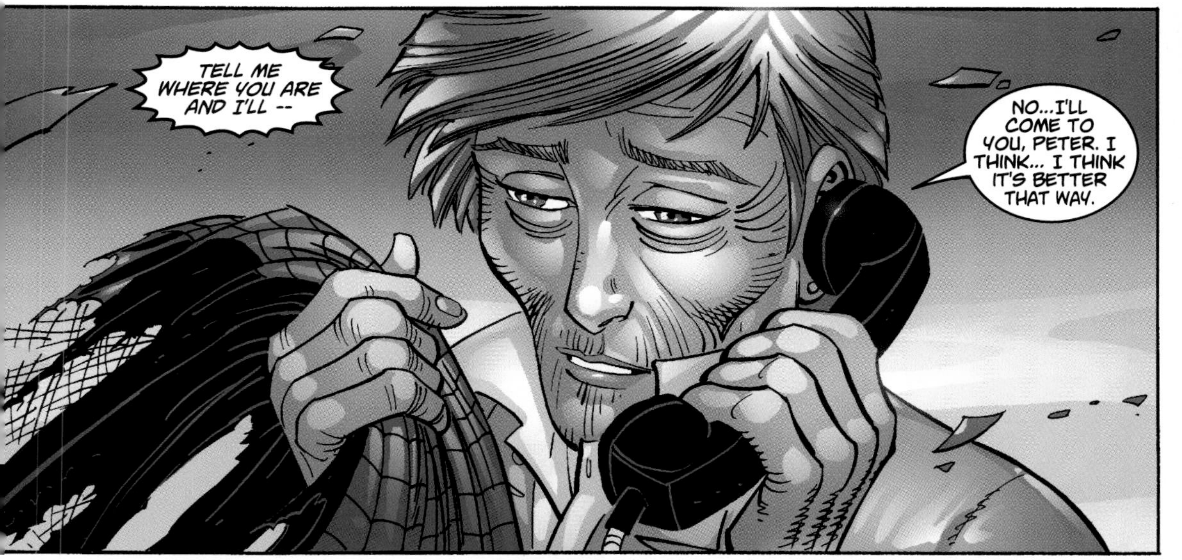
TELL ME WHERE YOU ARE AND I'LL --
NO...I'LL COME TO YOU, PETER. I THINK... I THINK IT'S BETTER THAT WAY.
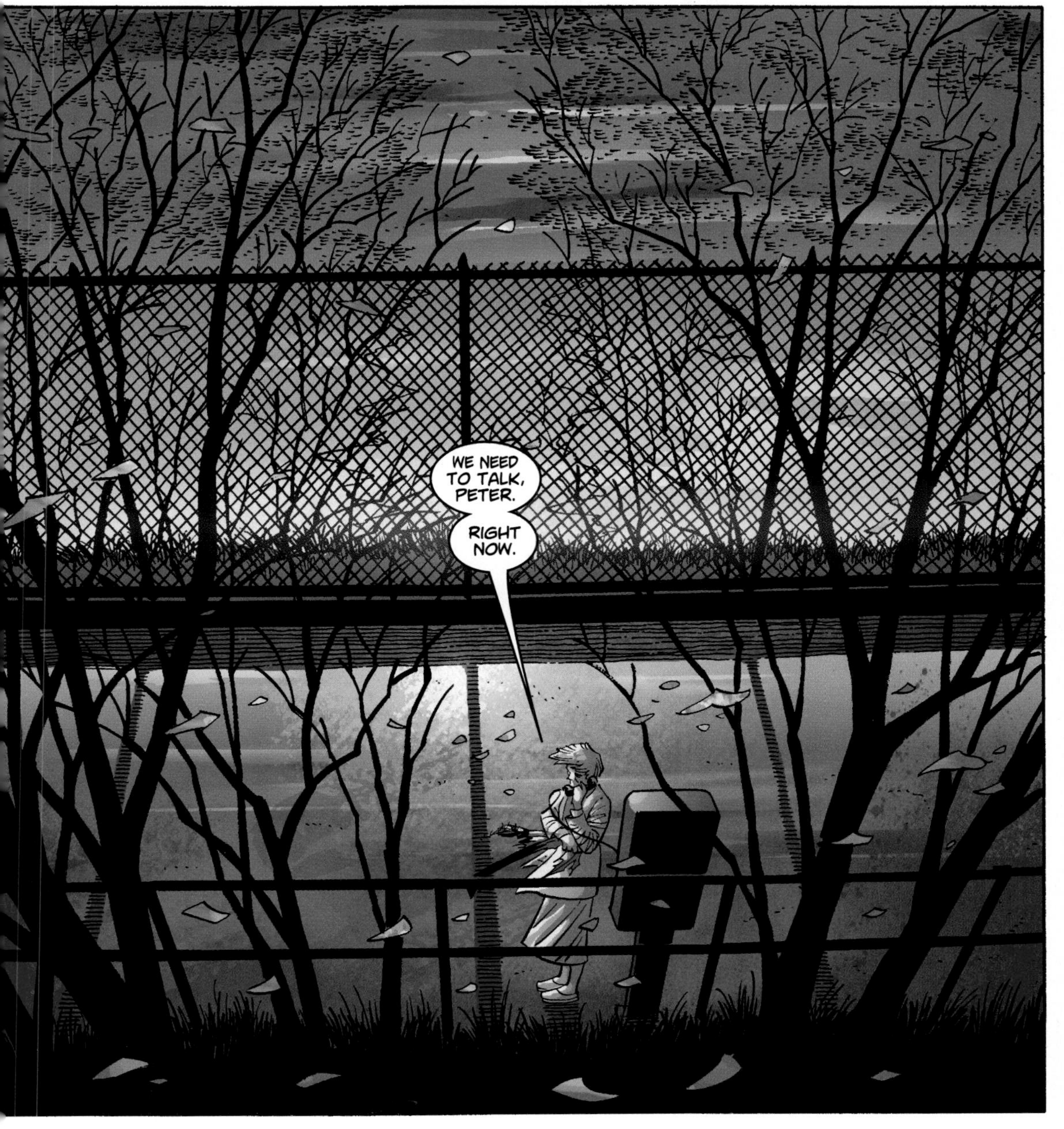
WE NEED TO TALK, PETER.
RIGHT NOW.

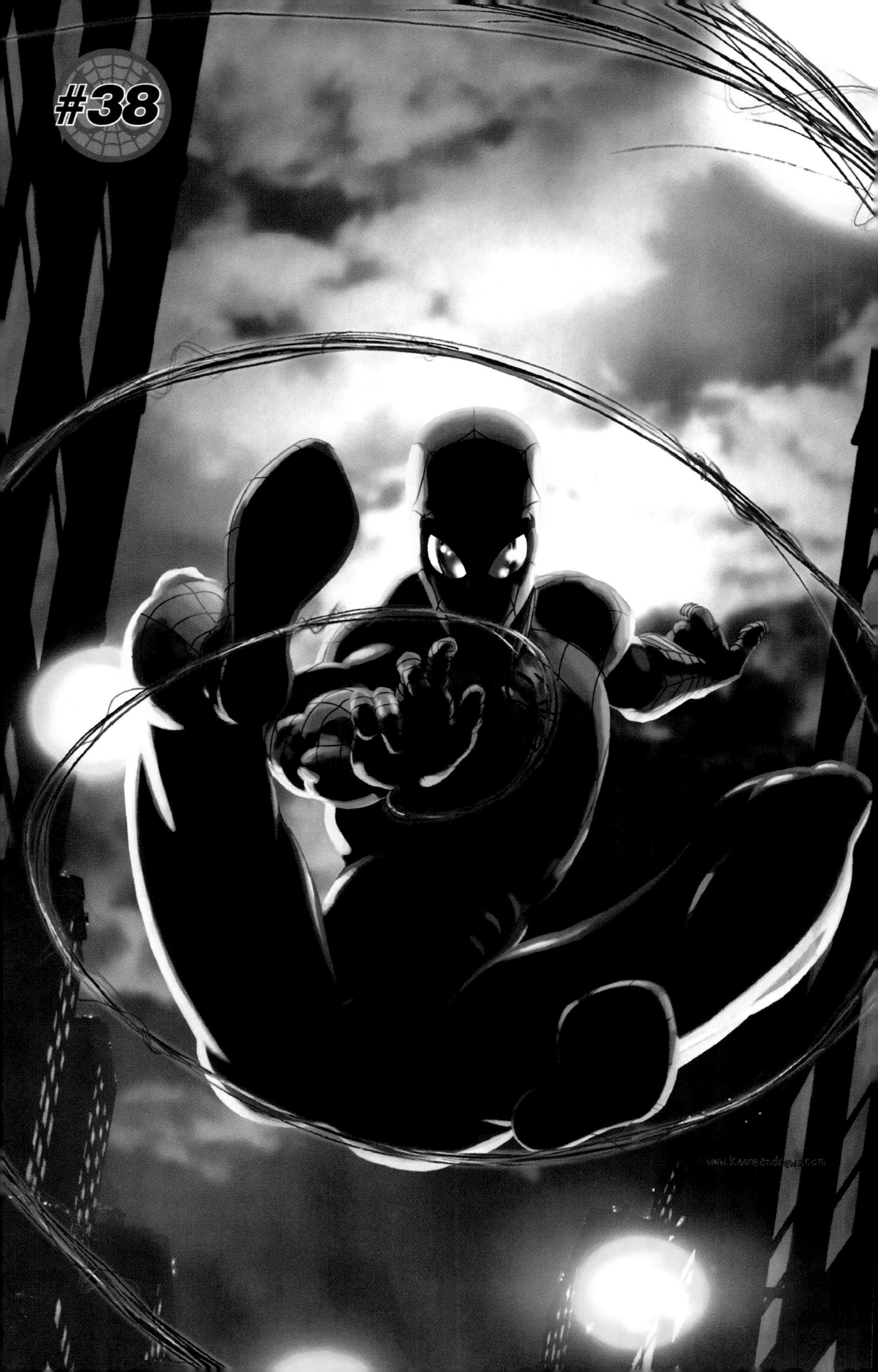
#38
www.kaareandrews.com

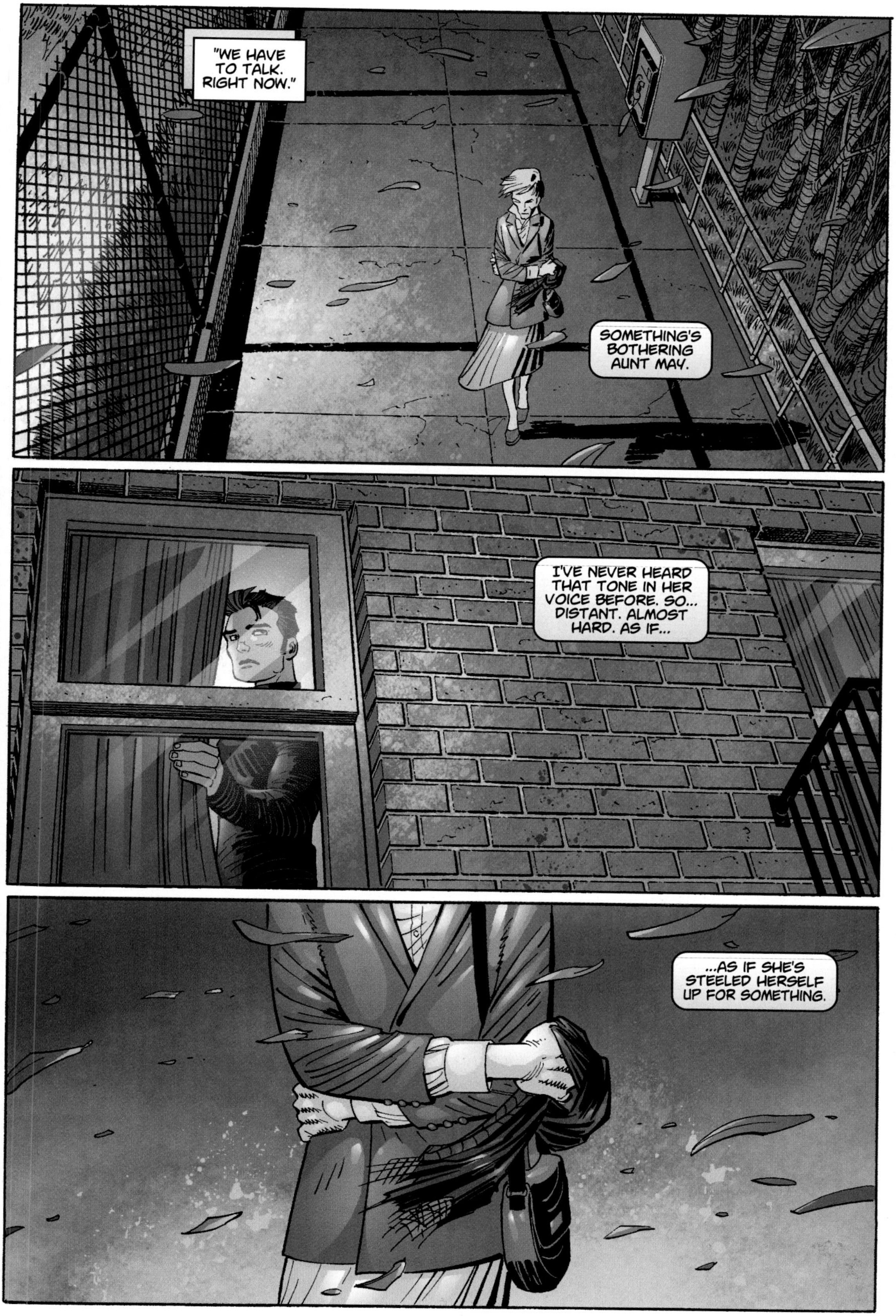
"WE HAVE TO TALK. RIGHT NOW."
SOMETHING'S BOTHERING AUNT MAY.
I'VE NEVER HEARD THAT TONE IN HER VOICE BEFORE. SO... DISTANT. ALMOST HARD. AS IF...
...AS IF SHE'S STEELED HERSELF UP FOR SOMETHING.

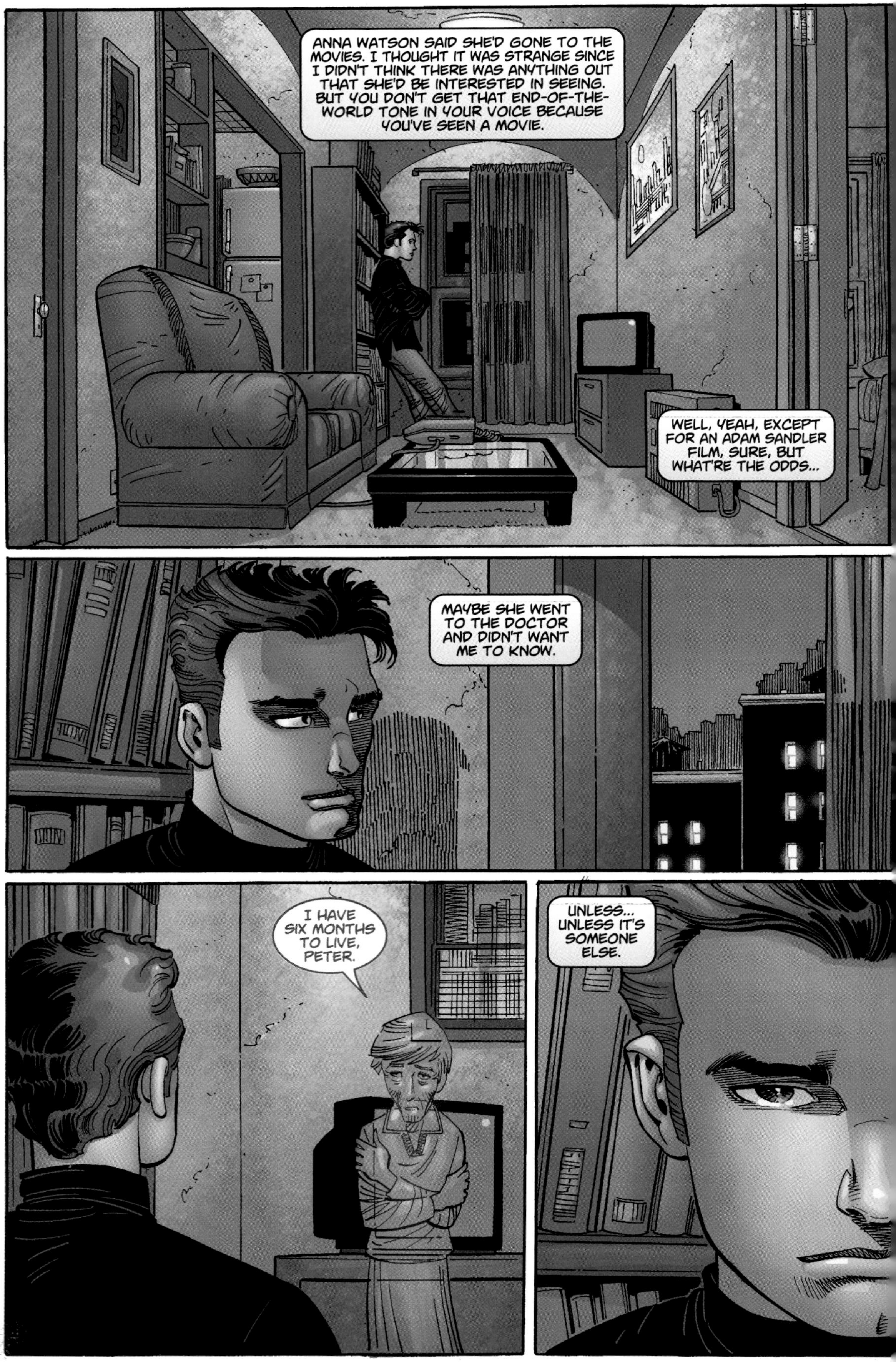
ANNA WATSON SAID SHE'D GONE TO THE MOVIES. I THOUGHT IT WAS STRANGE SINCE I DIDN'T THINK THERE WAS ANYTHING OUT THAT SHE'D BE INTERESTED IN SEEING. BUT YOU DON'T GET THAT END-OF-THE-WORLD TONE IN YOUR VOICE BECAUSE YOU'VE SEEN A MOVIE.
WELL, YEAH, EXCEPT FOR AN ADAM SANDLER FILM, SURE, BUT WHAT'RE THE ODDS...
MAYBE SHE WENT TO THE DOCTOR AND DIDN'T WANT ME TO KNOW.
I HAVE SIX MONTHS TO LIVE, PETER.
UNLESS... UNLESS IT'S SOMEONE ELSE.

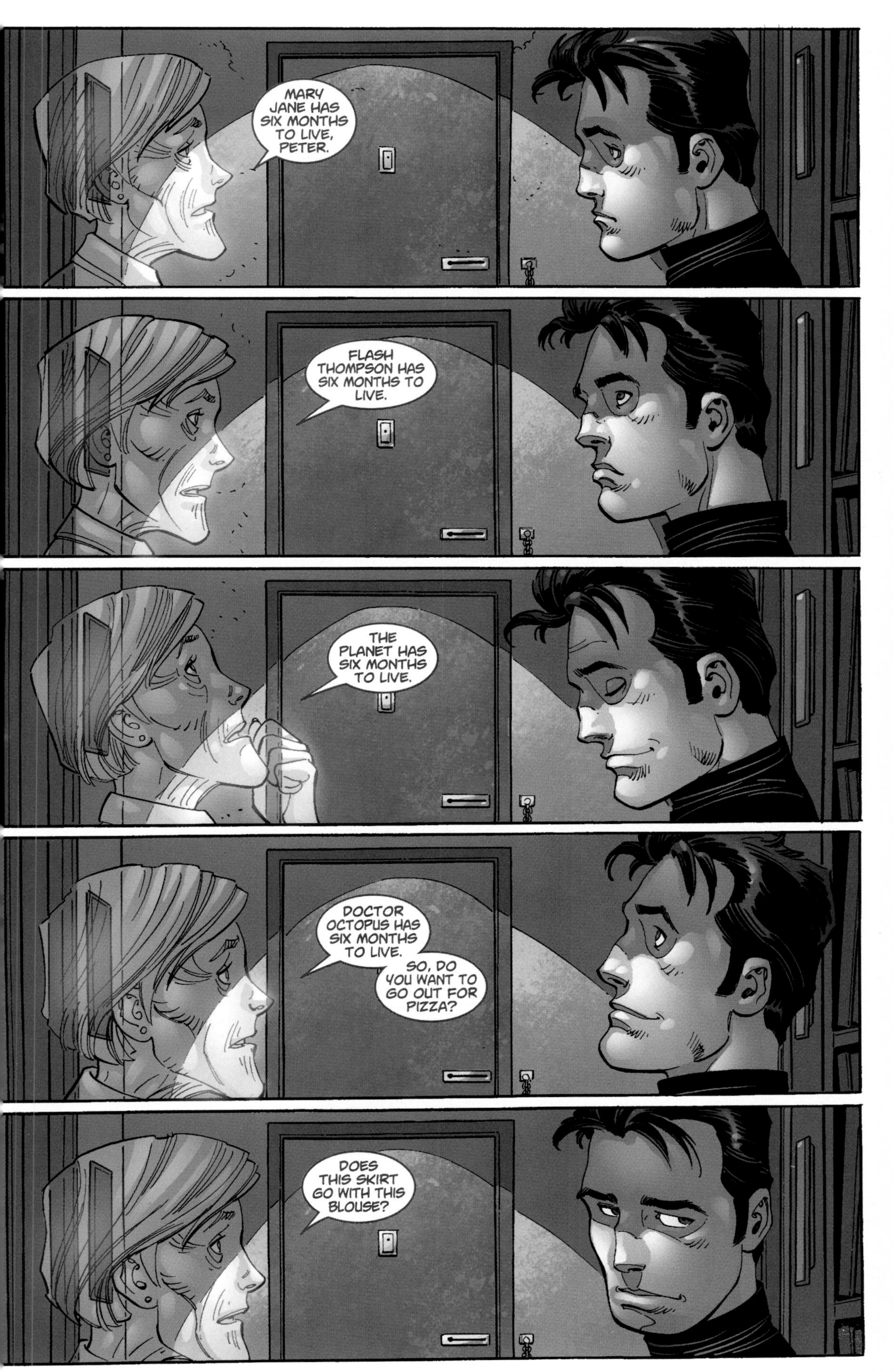
MARY JANE HAS SIX MONTHS TO LIVE, PETER.
FLASH THOMPSON HAS SIX MONTHS TO LIVE.
THE PLANET HAS SIX MONTHS TO LIVE.
DOCTOR OCTOPUS HAS SIX MONTHS TO LIVE.
SO, DO YOU WANT TO GO OUT FOR PIZZA?
DOES THIS SKIRT GO WITH THIS BLOUSE?

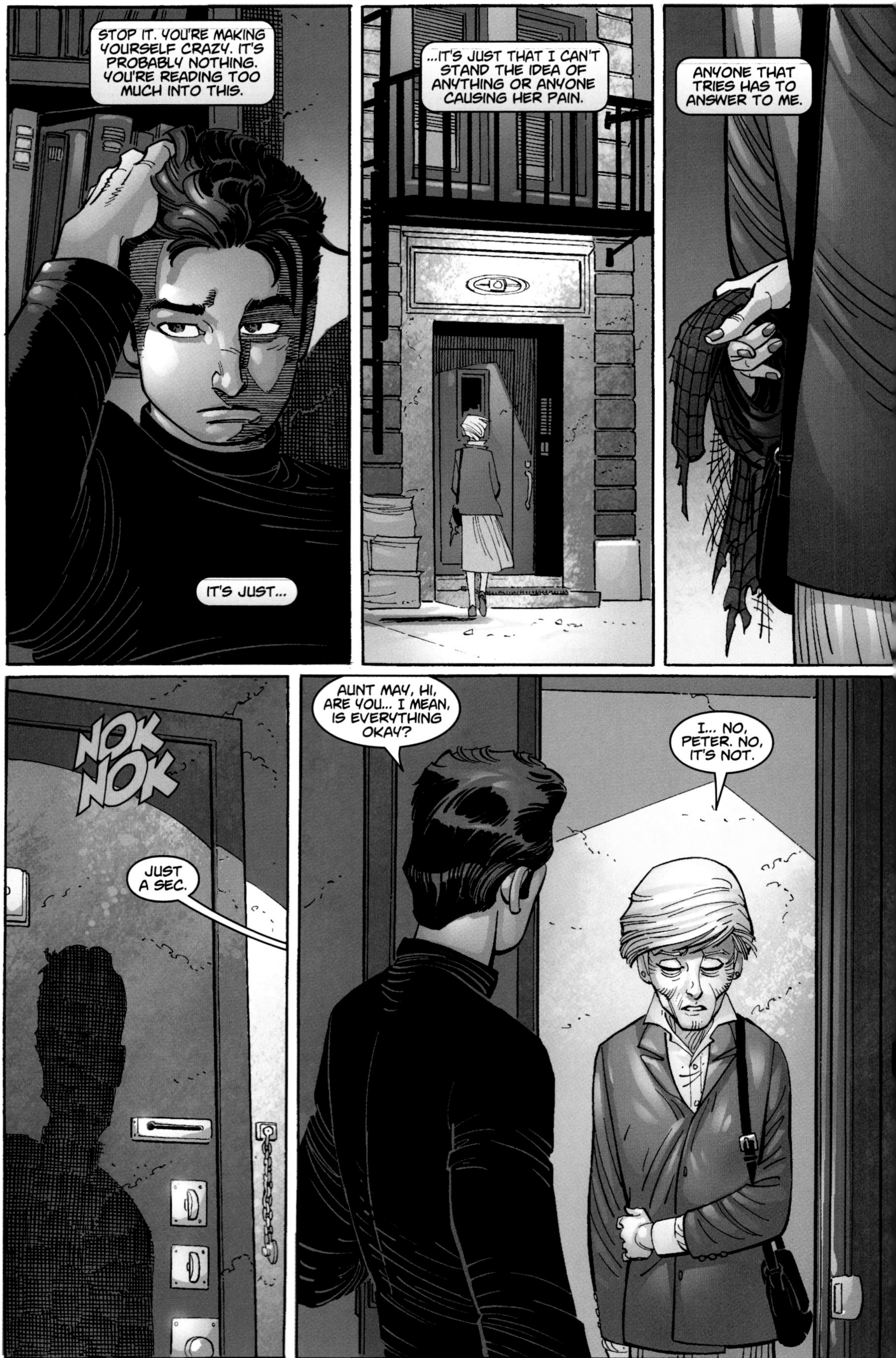
STOP IT. YOU'RE MAKING YOURSELF CRAZY. IT'S PROBABLY NOTHING. YOU'RE READING TOO MUCH INTO THIS.
IT'S JUST...
...IT'S JUST THAT I CAN'T STAND THE IDEA OF ANYTHING OR ANYONE CAUSING HER PAIN.
ANYONE THAT TRIES HAS TO ANSWER TO ME.
NOK NOK
JUST A SEC.
AUNT MAY, HI, ARE YOU... I MEAN, IS EVERYTHING OKAY?
I... NO, PETER. NO, IT'S NOT.

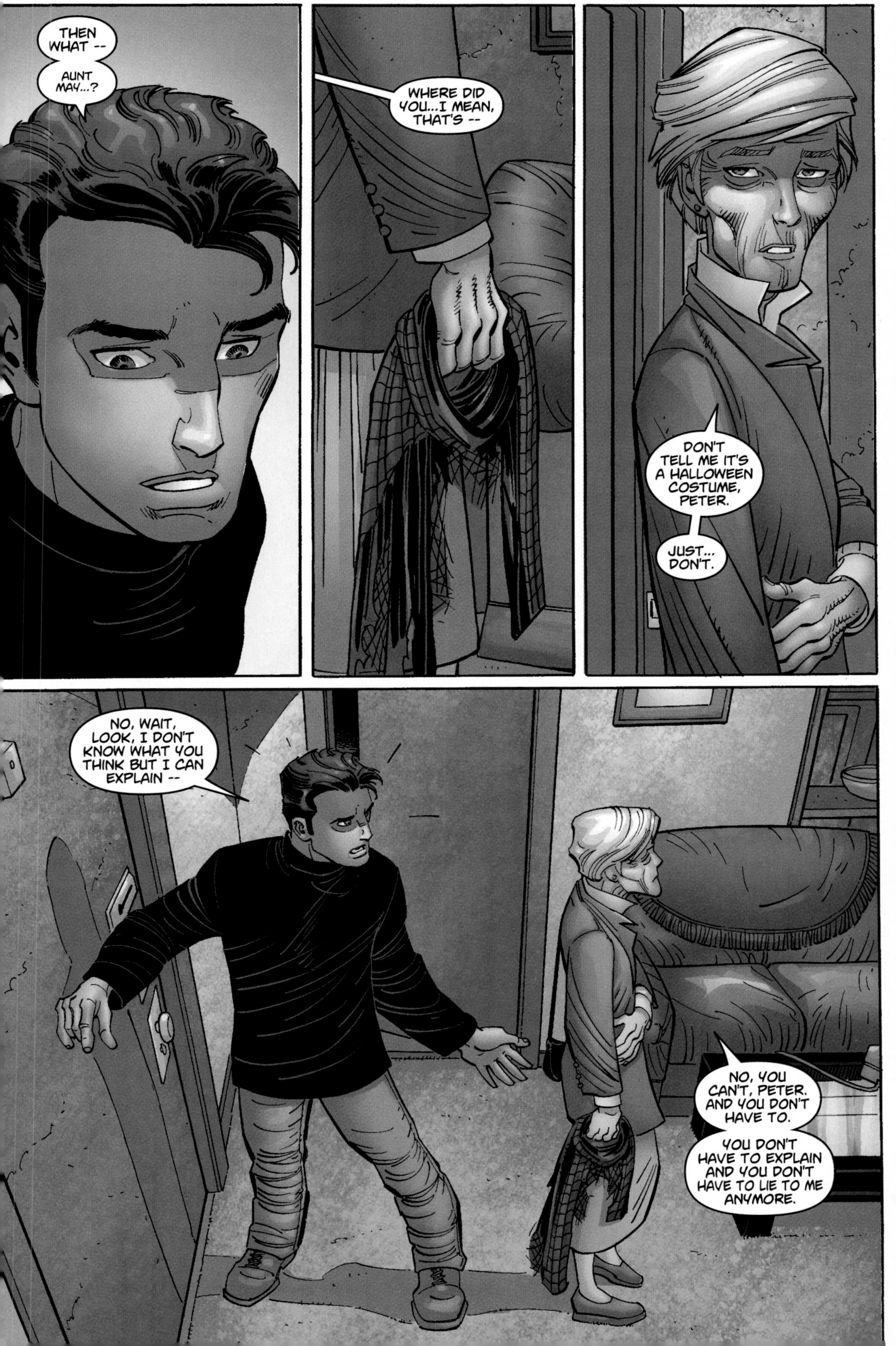
THEN WHAT --
AUNT MAY...?
WHERE DID YOU...I MEAN, THAT'S --
DON'T TELL ME IT'S A HALLOWEEN COSTUME, PETER.
JUST... DON'T.
NO, WAIT, LOOK, I DON'T KNOW WHAT YOU THINK BUT I CAN EXPLAIN --
NO, YOU CAN'T, PETER. AND YOU DON'T HAVE TO.
YOU DON'T HAVE TO EXPLAIN AND YOU DON'T HAVE TO LIE TO ME ANYMORE.

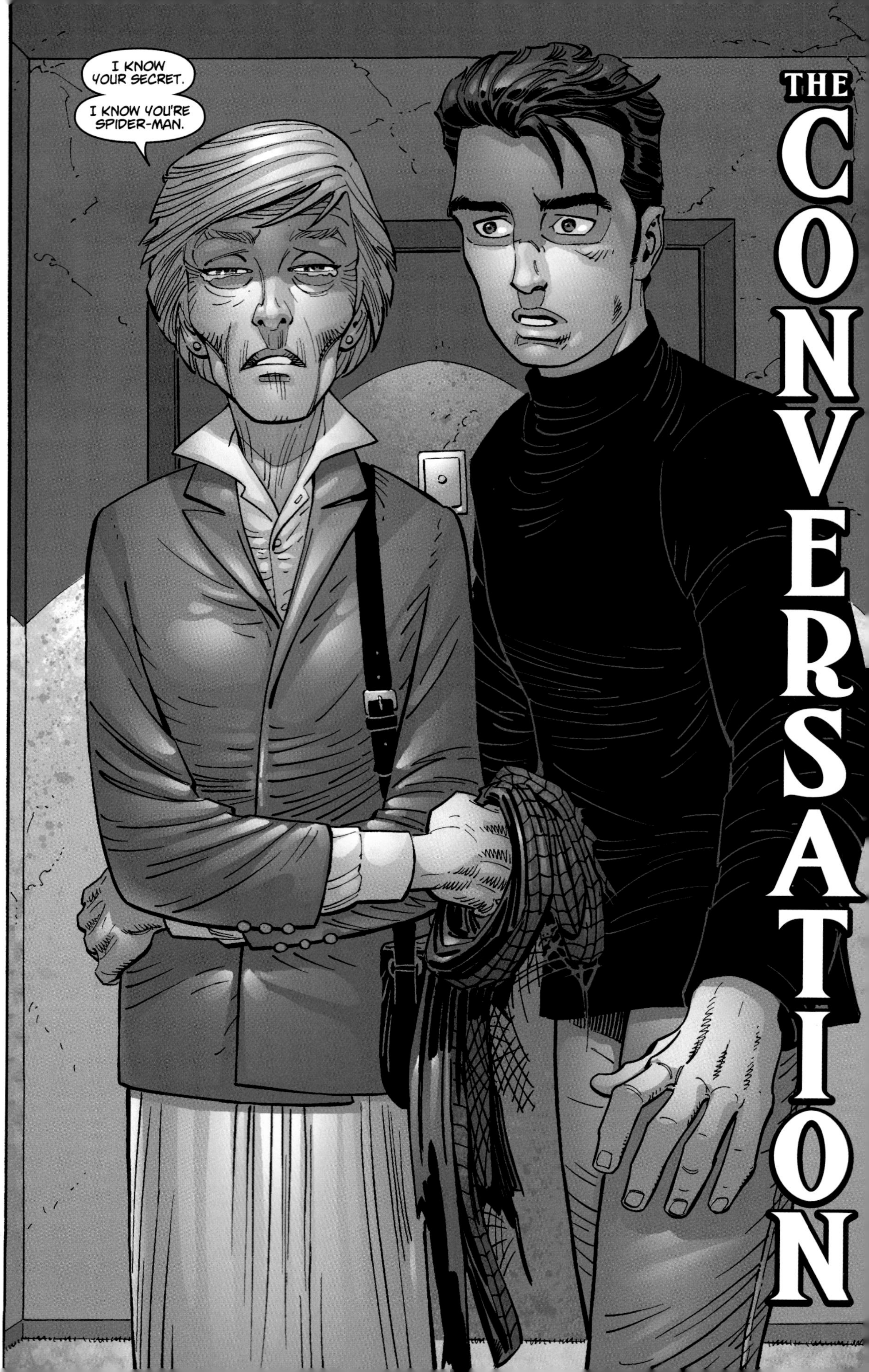
I KNOW YOUR SECRET.
I KNOW YOU'RE SPIDER-MAN.
THE CONVERSATION

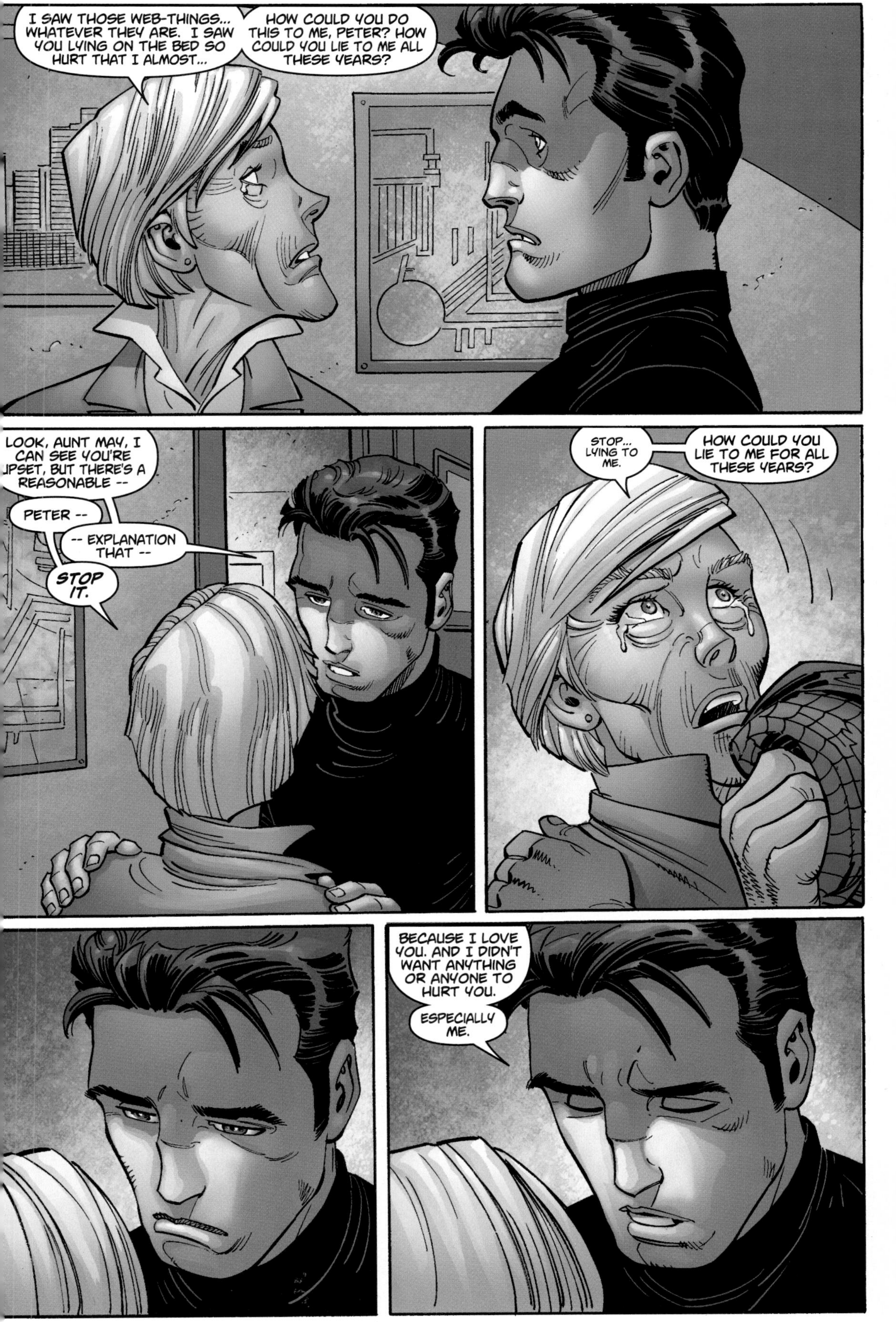
I SAW THOSE WEB-THINGS... WHATEVER THEY ARE. I SAW YOU LYING ON THE BED SO HURT THAT I ALMOST...
HOW COULD YOU DO THIS TO ME, PETER? HOW COULD YOU LIE TO ME ALL THESE YEARS?
LOOK, AUNT MAY, I CAN SEE YOU'RE UPSET, BUT THERE'S A REASONABLE --
PETER --
-- EXPLANATION THAT --
STOP IT.
STOP... LYING TO ME.
HOW COULD YOU LIE TO ME FOR ALL THESE YEARS?
BECAUSE I LOVE YOU. AND I DIDN'T WANT ANYTHING OR ANYONE TO HURT YOU.
ESPECIALLY ME.

WHAT DID YOU THINK WOULD HAPPEN IF I FOUND OUT, PETER? DID YOU THINK I WOULD JUST KEEL OVER AND DIE?

AUNT MAY --

WHEN YOUR PARENTS DIED, I RAISED YOU. I CARRIED THAT BURDEN AND IT NEVER BROKE ME, THOUGH THERE WERE TIMES I THOUGHT IT MIGHT.

WHEN YOUR UNCLE BEN DIED, AND MOST OF MY WORLD DIED WITH HIM, IT WOULD HAVE BEEN EASY TO JUST GIVE UP, TO ROLL OVER AND DIE. BUT YOU NEEDED ME, SO I DEALT WITH IT AND KEPT GOING.

I HAVE BURIED FRIENDS AND LOVED ONES AND RELATIVES. I HAVE WATCHED YOU SUFFER OVER YOUR OWN LOSSES, KNOWING THERE WAS NOTHING I COULD DO BUT BE THERE WHEN YOU NEEDED ME.

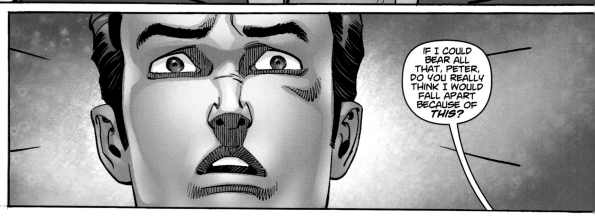

IF I COULD BEAR ALL THAT, PETER, DO YOU REALLY THINK I WOULD FALL APART BECAUSE OF *THIS*?

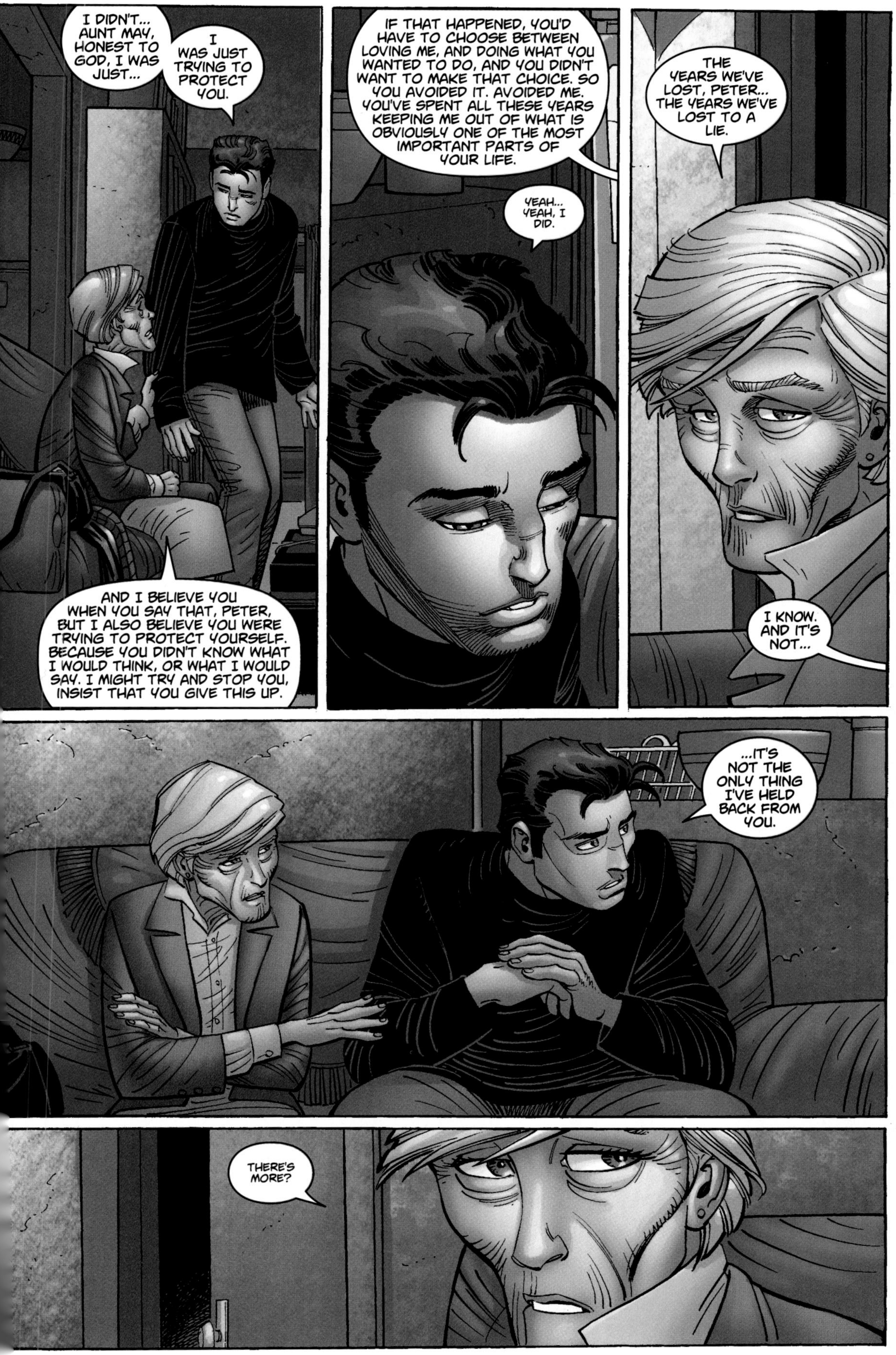
I DIDN'T... AUNT MAY, HONEST TO GOD, I WAS JUST...
I WAS JUST TRYING TO PROTECT YOU.
AND I BELIEVE YOU WHEN YOU SAY THAT, PETER, BUT I ALSO BELIEVE YOU WERE TRYING TO PROTECT YOURSELF. BECAUSE YOU DIDN'T KNOW WHAT I WOULD THINK, OR WHAT I WOULD SAY. I MIGHT TRY AND STOP YOU, INSIST THAT YOU GIVE THIS UP.
IF THAT HAPPENED, YOU'D HAVE TO CHOOSE BETWEEN LOVING ME, AND DOING WHAT YOU WANTED TO DO, AND YOU DIDN'T WANT TO MAKE THAT CHOICE. SO YOU AVOIDED IT. AVOIDED ME. YOU'VE SPENT ALL THESE YEARS KEEPING ME OUT OF WHAT IS OBVIOUSLY ONE OF THE MOST IMPORTANT PARTS OF YOUR LIFE.
YEAH... YEAH, I DID.
THE YEARS WE'VE LOST, PETER... THE YEARS WE'VE LOST TO A LIE.
I KNOW. AND IT'S NOT...
...IT'S NOT THE ONLY THING I'VE HELD BACK FROM YOU.
THERE'S MORE?

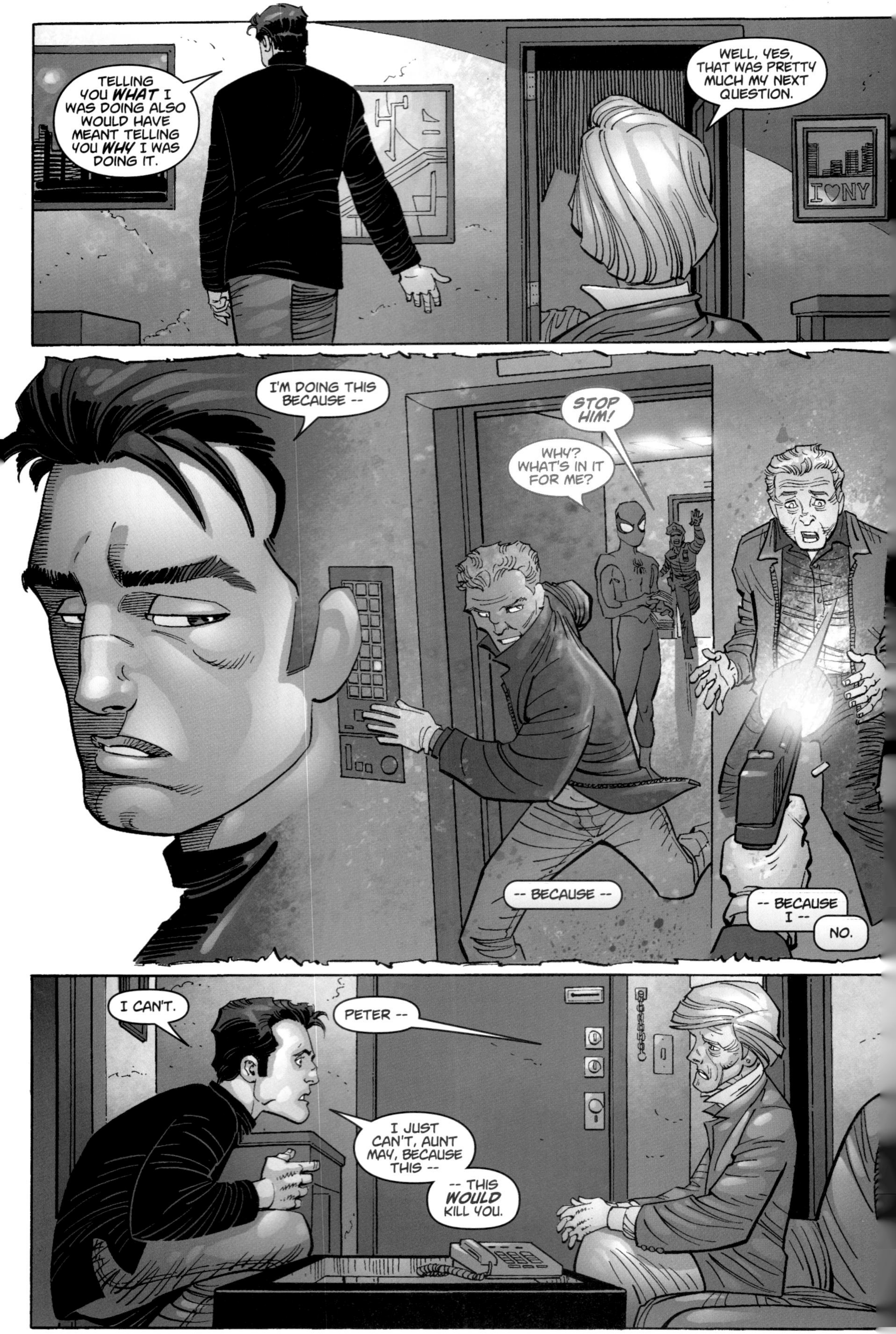
TELLING YOU *WHAT* I WAS DOING ALSO WOULD HAVE MEANT TELLING YOU *WHY* I WAS DOING IT.
WELL, YES, THAT WAS PRETTY MUCH MY NEXT QUESTION.
I♥NY
I'M DOING THIS BECAUSE --
STOP HIM!
WHY? WHAT'S IN IT FOR ME?
-- BECAUSE --
-- BECAUSE I --
NO.
I CAN'T.
PETER --
I JUST CAN'T, AUNT MAY, BECAUSE THIS --
-- THIS *WOULD* KILL YOU.

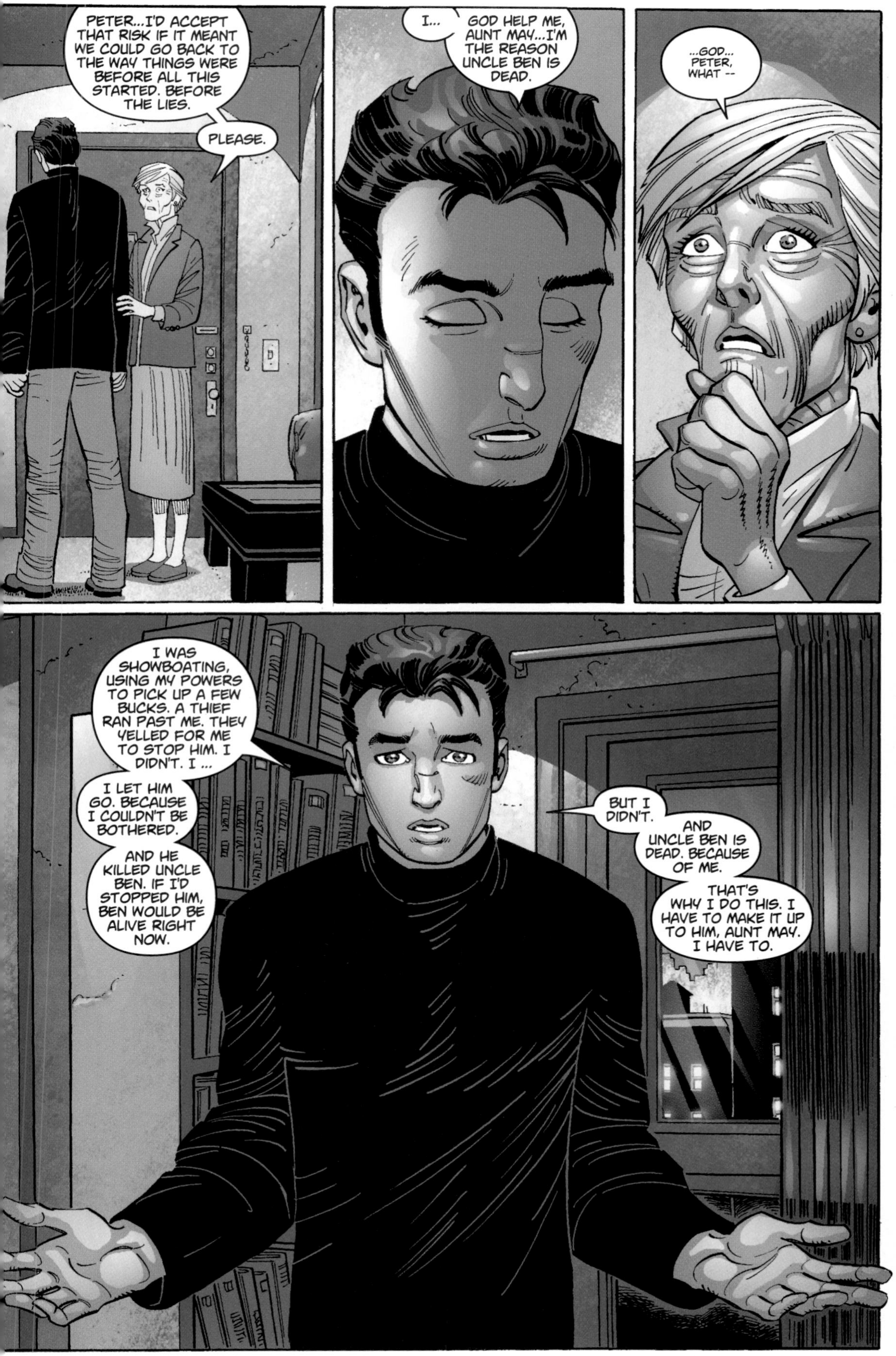
PETER...I'D ACCEPT THAT RISK IF IT MEANT WE COULD GO BACK TO THE WAY THINGS WERE BEFORE ALL THIS STARTED. BEFORE THE LIES.
PLEASE.
I...
GOD HELP ME, AUNT MAY...I'M THE REASON UNCLE BEN IS DEAD.
...GOD... PETER, WHAT --
I WAS SHOWBOATING, USING MY POWERS TO PICK UP A FEW BUCKS. A THIEF RAN PAST ME. THEY YELLED FOR ME TO STOP HIM. I DIDN'T. I ...
I LET HIM GO. BECAUSE I COULDN'T BE BOTHERED.
AND HE KILLED UNCLE BEN. IF I'D STOPPED HIM, BEN WOULD BE ALIVE RIGHT NOW.
BUT I DIDN'T.
AND UNCLE BEN IS DEAD. BECAUSE OF ME.
THAT'S WHY I DO THIS. I HAVE TO MAKE IT UP TO HIM, AUNT MAY. I HAVE TO.

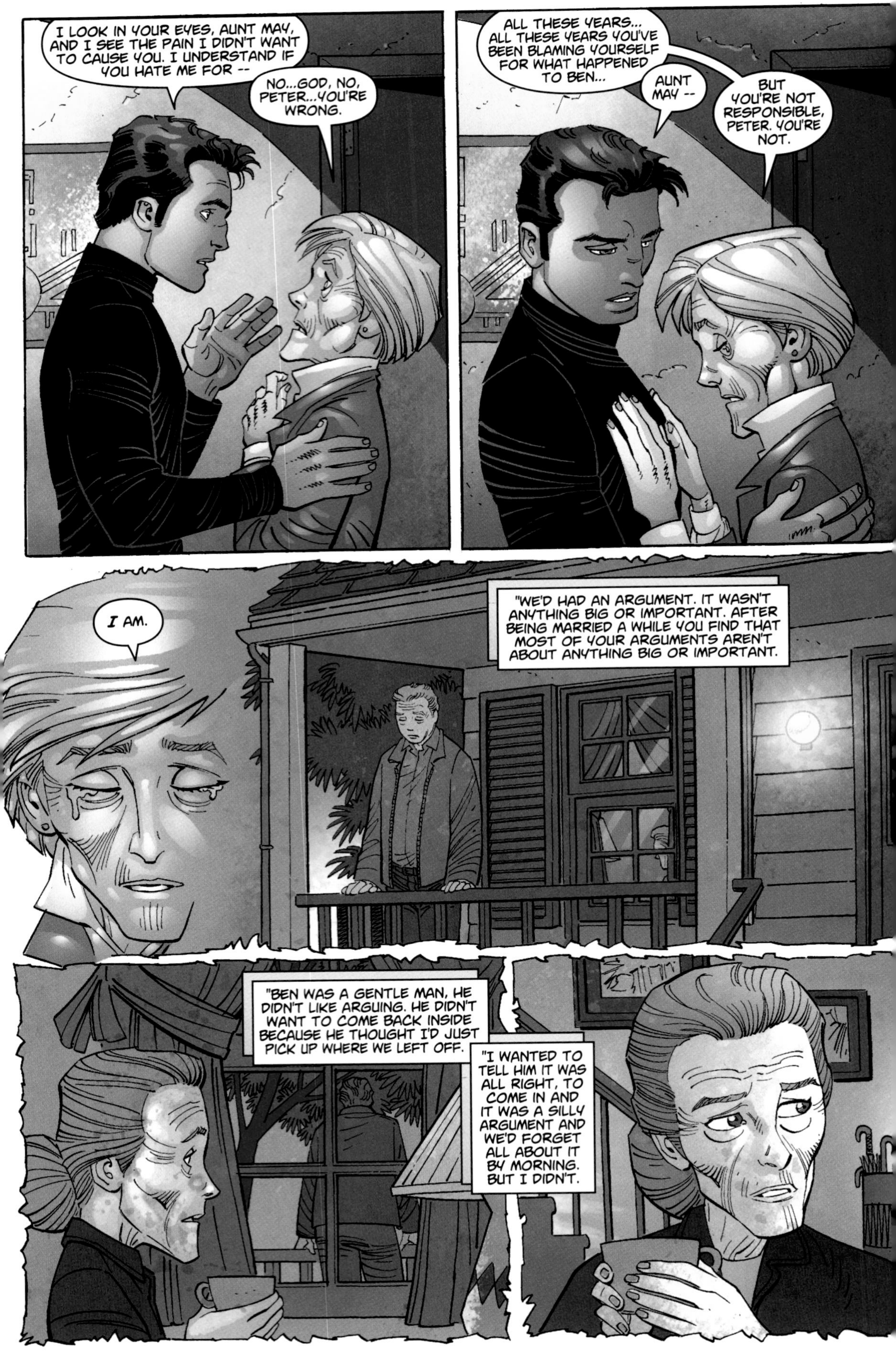
I LOOK IN YOUR EYES, AUNT MAY, AND I SEE THE PAIN I DIDN'T WANT TO CAUSE YOU. I UNDERSTAND IF YOU HATE ME FOR --
NO...GOD, NO, PETER...YOU'RE WRONG.
ALL THESE YEARS... ALL THESE YEARS YOU'VE BEEN BLAMING YOURSELF FOR WHAT HAPPENED TO BEN...
AUNT MAY --
BUT YOU'RE NOT RESPONSIBLE, PETER. YOU'RE NOT.
I AM.
"WE'D HAD AN ARGUMENT. IT WASN'T ANYTHING BIG OR IMPORTANT. AFTER BEING MARRIED A WHILE YOU FIND THAT MOST OF YOUR ARGUMENTS AREN'T ABOUT ANYTHING BIG OR IMPORTANT.
"BEN WAS A GENTLE MAN, HE DIDN'T LIKE ARGUING. HE DIDN'T WANT TO COME BACK INSIDE BECAUSE HE THOUGHT I'D JUST PICK UP WHERE WE LEFT OFF.
"I WANTED TO TELL HIM IT WAS ALL RIGHT, TO COME IN AND IT WAS A SILLY ARGUMENT AND WE'D FORGET ALL ABOUT IT BY MORNING. BUT I DIDN'T.

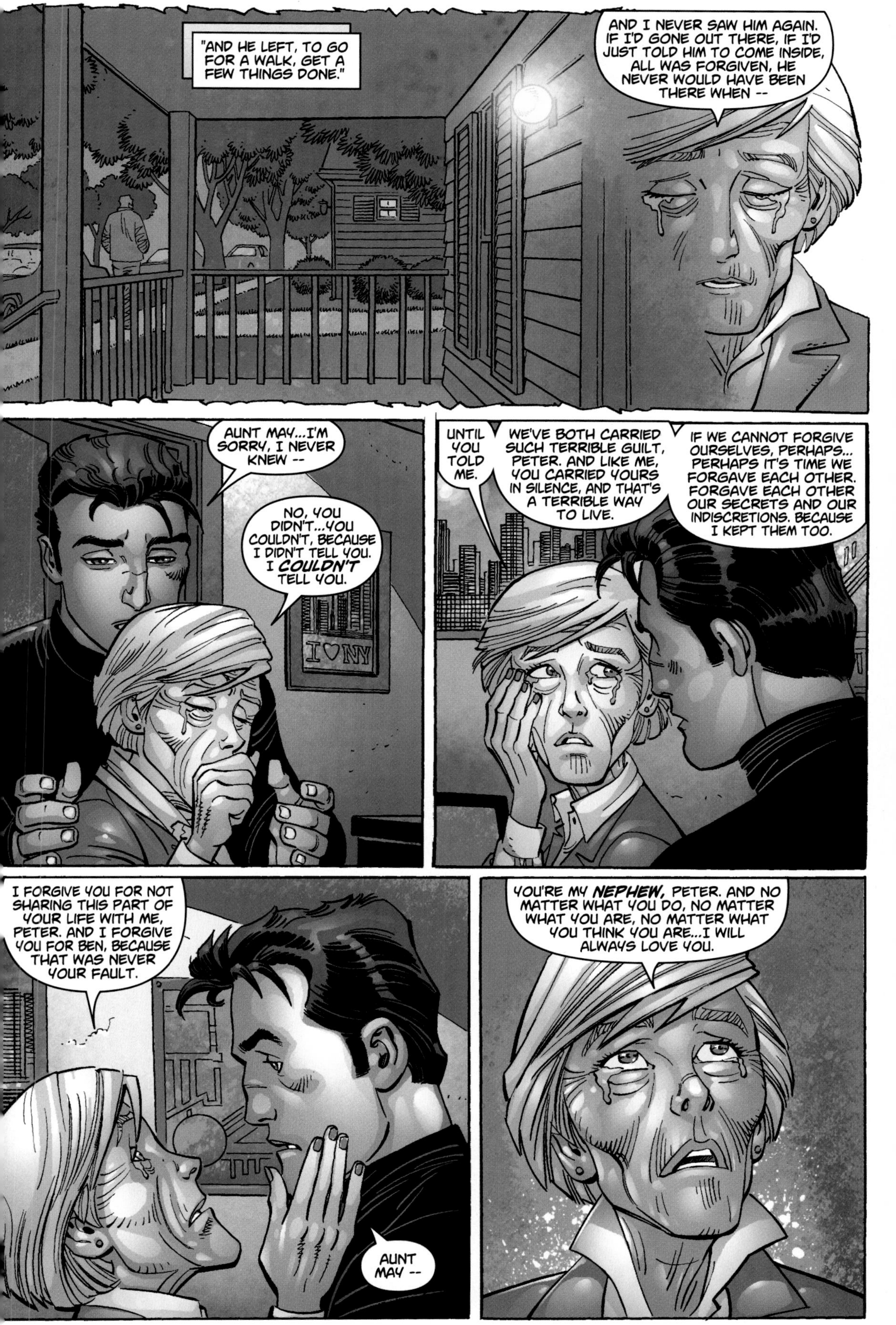
"AND HE LEFT, TO GO FOR A WALK, GET A FEW THINGS DONE."
AND I NEVER SAW HIM AGAIN. IF I'D GONE OUT THERE, IF I'D JUST TOLD HIM TO COME INSIDE, ALL WAS FORGIVEN, HE NEVER WOULD HAVE BEEN THERE WHEN --
AUNT MAY...I'M SORRY, I NEVER KNEW --
NO, YOU DIDN'T...YOU COULDN'T, BECAUSE I DIDN'T TELL YOU. I ***COULDN'T*** TELL YOU.
I ♥ NY
UNTIL YOU TOLD ME.
WE'VE BOTH CARRIED SUCH TERRIBLE GUILT, PETER. AND LIKE ME, YOU CARRIED YOURS IN SILENCE, AND THAT'S A TERRIBLE WAY TO LIVE.
IF WE CANNOT FORGIVE OURSELVES, PERHAPS... PERHAPS IT'S TIME WE FORGAVE EACH OTHER. FORGAVE EACH OTHER OUR SECRETS AND OUR INDISCRETIONS. BECAUSE I KEPT THEM TOO.
I FORGIVE YOU FOR NOT SHARING THIS PART OF YOUR LIFE WITH ME, PETER. AND I FORGIVE YOU FOR BEN, BECAUSE THAT WAS NEVER YOUR FAULT.
AUNT MAY --
YOU'RE MY ***NEPHEW,*** PETER. AND NO MATTER WHAT YOU DO, NO MATTER WHAT YOU ARE, NO MATTER WHAT YOU THINK YOU ARE...I WILL ALWAYS LOVE YOU.

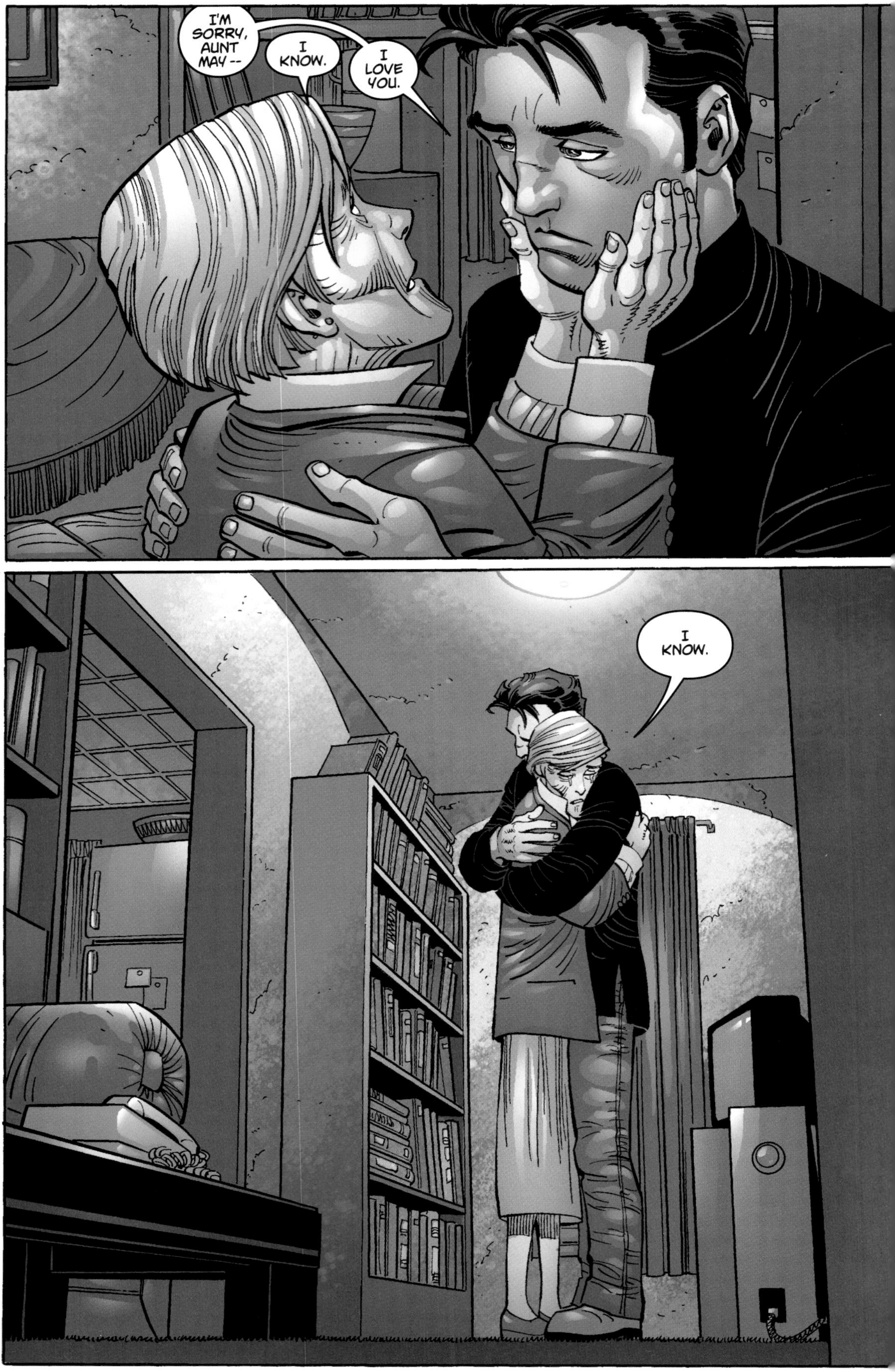
I'M SORRY, AUNT MAY --
I KNOW.
I LOVE YOU.
I KNOW.

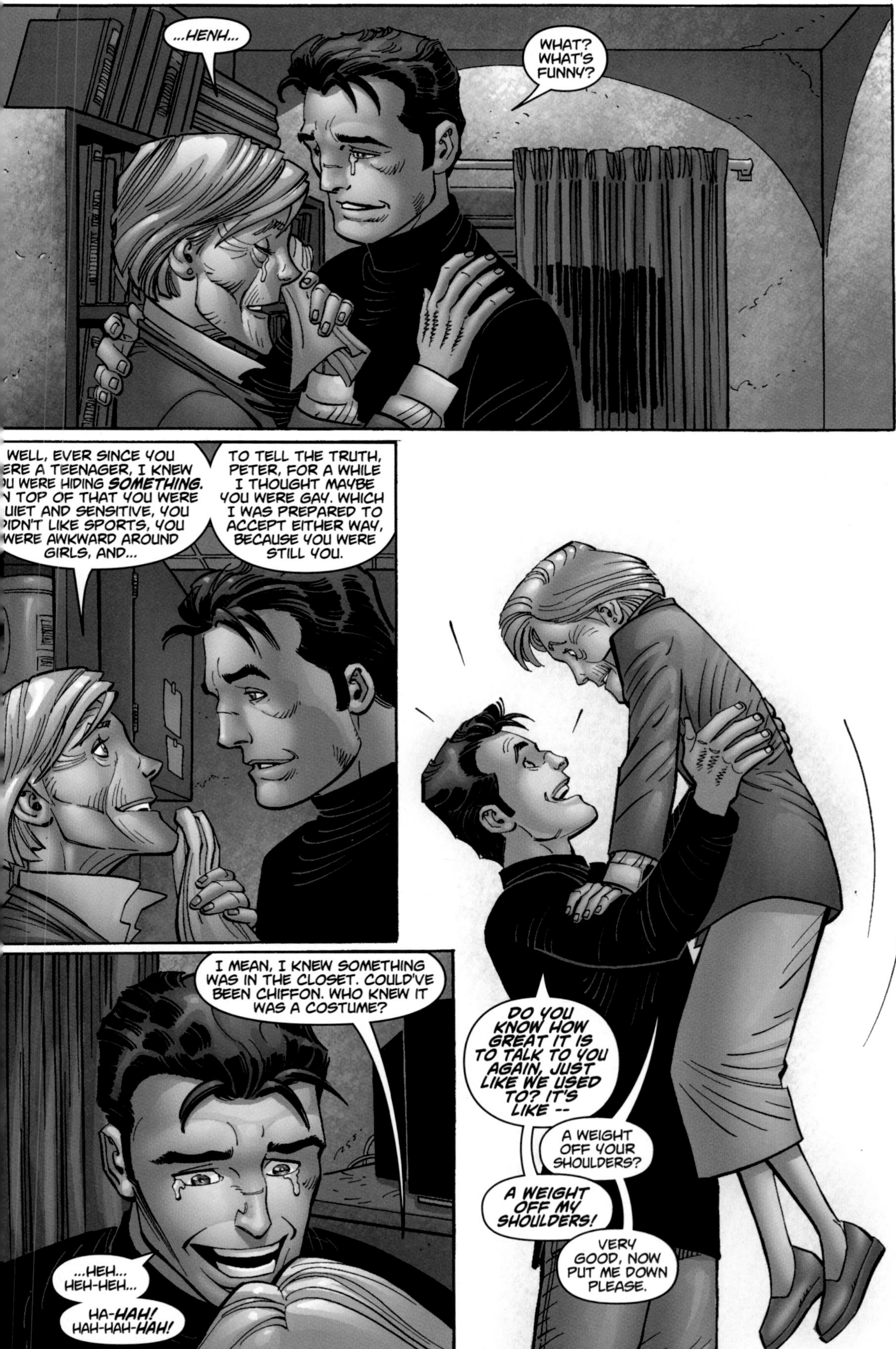
...HENH...
WHAT? WHAT'S FUNNY?
WELL, EVER SINCE YOU ERE A TEENAGER, I KNEW OU WERE HIDING SOMETHING. N TOP OF THAT YOU WERE UIET AND SENSITIVE, YOU IDN'T LIKE SPORTS, YOU WERE AWKWARD AROUND GIRLS, AND...
TO TELL THE TRUTH, PETER, FOR A WHILE I THOUGHT MAYBE YOU WERE GAY. WHICH I WAS PREPARED TO ACCEPT EITHER WAY, BECAUSE YOU WERE STILL YOU.
I MEAN, I KNEW SOMETHING WAS IN THE CLOSET. COULD'VE BEEN CHIFFON. WHO KNEW IT WAS A COSTUME?
...HEH... HEH-HEH...
HA-HAH! HAH-HAH-HAH!
DO YOU KNOW HOW GREAT IT IS TO TALK TO YOU AGAIN, JUST LIKE WE USED TO? IT'S LIKE --
A WEIGHT OFF YOUR SHOULDERS?
A WEIGHT OFF MY SHOULDERS!
VERY GOOD, NOW PUT ME DOWN PLEASE.

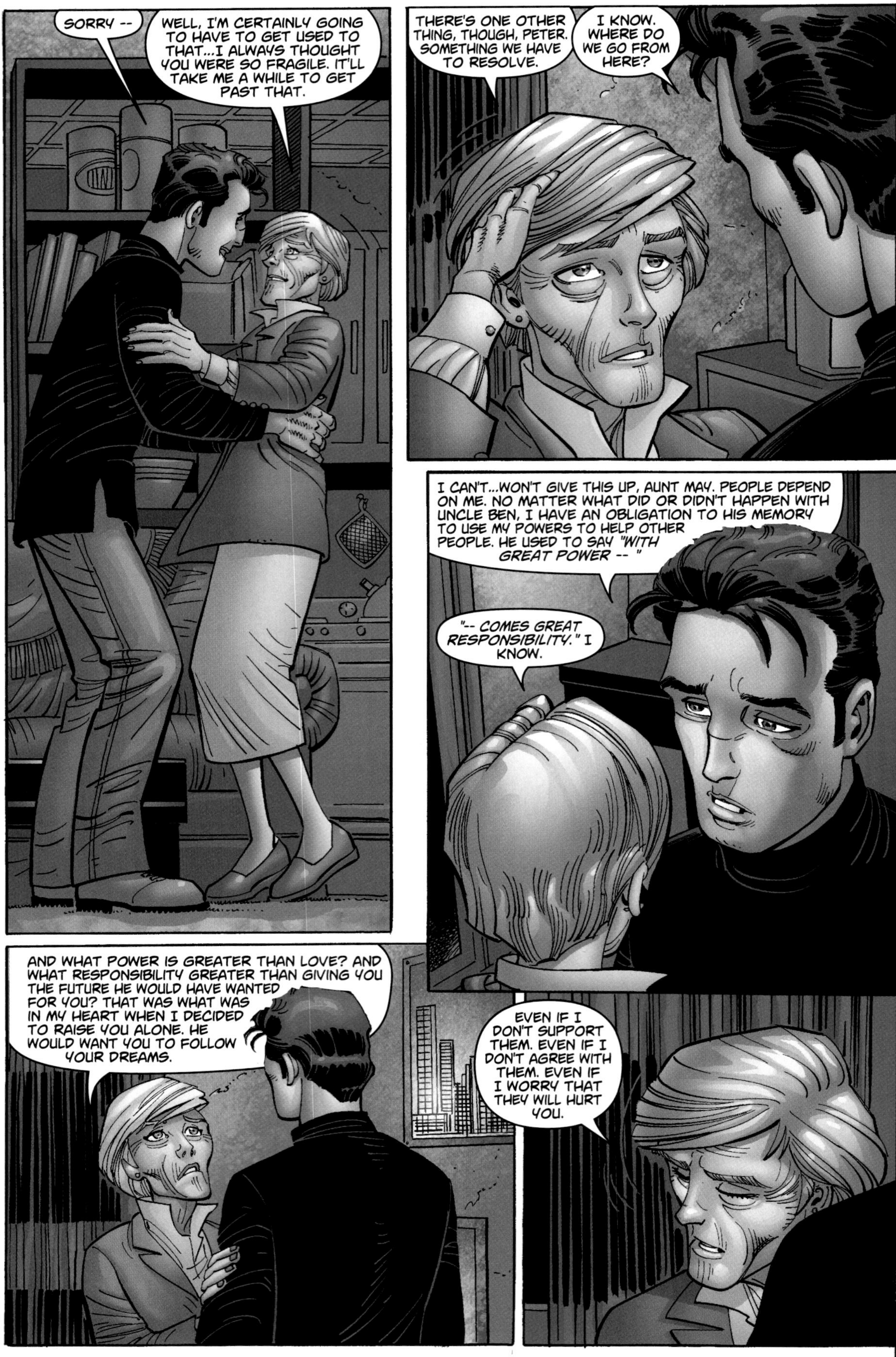
SORRY --
WELL, I'M CERTAINLY GOING TO HAVE TO GET USED TO THAT...I ALWAYS THOUGHT YOU WERE SO FRAGILE. IT'LL TAKE ME A WHILE TO GET PAST THAT.
THERE'S ONE OTHER THING, THOUGH, PETER. SOMETHING WE HAVE TO RESOLVE.
I KNOW. WHERE DO WE GO FROM HERE?
I CAN'T...WON'T GIVE THIS UP, AUNT MAY. PEOPLE DEPEND ON ME. NO MATTER WHAT DID OR DIDN'T HAPPEN WITH UNCLE BEN, I HAVE AN OBLIGATION TO HIS MEMORY TO USE MY POWERS TO HELP OTHER PEOPLE. HE USED TO SAY "WITH GREAT POWER -- "
"-- COMES GREAT RESPONSIBILITY." I KNOW.
AND WHAT POWER IS GREATER THAN LOVE? AND WHAT RESPONSIBILITY GREATER THAN GIVING YOU THE FUTURE HE WOULD HAVE WANTED FOR YOU? THAT WAS WHAT WAS IN MY HEART WHEN I DECIDED TO RAISE YOU ALONE. HE WOULD WANT YOU TO FOLLOW YOUR DREAMS.
EVEN IF I DON'T SUPPORT THEM. EVEN IF I DON'T AGREE WITH THEM. EVEN IF I WORRY THAT THEY WILL HURT YOU.

PETER, I'M OLDER THAN I EVER THOUGHT I WOULD BE. I'VE OUTLIVED ALMOST EVERYONE I KNEW AS A CHILD. AND I'VE LEARNED A FEW THINGS. THE MAIN THING I'VE LEARNED IS THAT YOU HAVE TO LET PEOPLE FIND THEIR OWN WAY, EVEN IF IT MEANS THEY GET HURT ALONG THE WAY.

SO I WON'T STOP YOU. I DON'T THINK I COULD STOP YOU EVEN IF I TRIED. IF I DID YOU'D EITHER GO ALONG AND HATE ME, OR SPIDER-MAN WOULD GO AWAY AND SOMEBODY ELSE WOULD APPEAR, AND WE'D JUST GO BACK TO LYING TO EACH OTHER AGAIN.

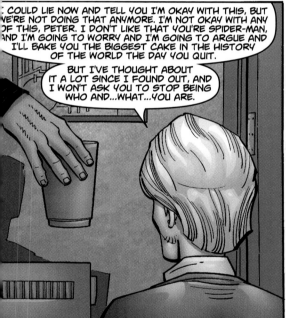

I COULD LIE NOW AND TELL YOU I'M OKAY WITH THIS, BUT WE'RE NOT DOING THAT ANYMORE. I'M NOT OKAY WITH ANY OF THIS, PETER. I DON'T LIKE THAT YOU'RE SPIDER-MAN, AND I'M GOING TO WORRY AND I'M GOING TO ARGUE AND I'LL BAKE YOU THE BIGGEST CAKE IN THE HISTORY OF THE WORLD THE DAY YOU QUIT.

BUT I'VE THOUGHT ABOUT IT A LOT SINCE I FOUND OUT, AND I WON'T ASK YOU TO STOP BEING WHO AND...WHAT...YOU ARE.

THERE'S JUST ONE THING I *DO* WANT TO KNOW.

ANYTHING.

HOW DID THIS HAPPEN? BECAUSE I DON'T THINK THERE'S ANY OF THIS SORT OF THING ON EITHER SIDE OF YOUR FAMILY.

IT'S... A *LONG* STORY.

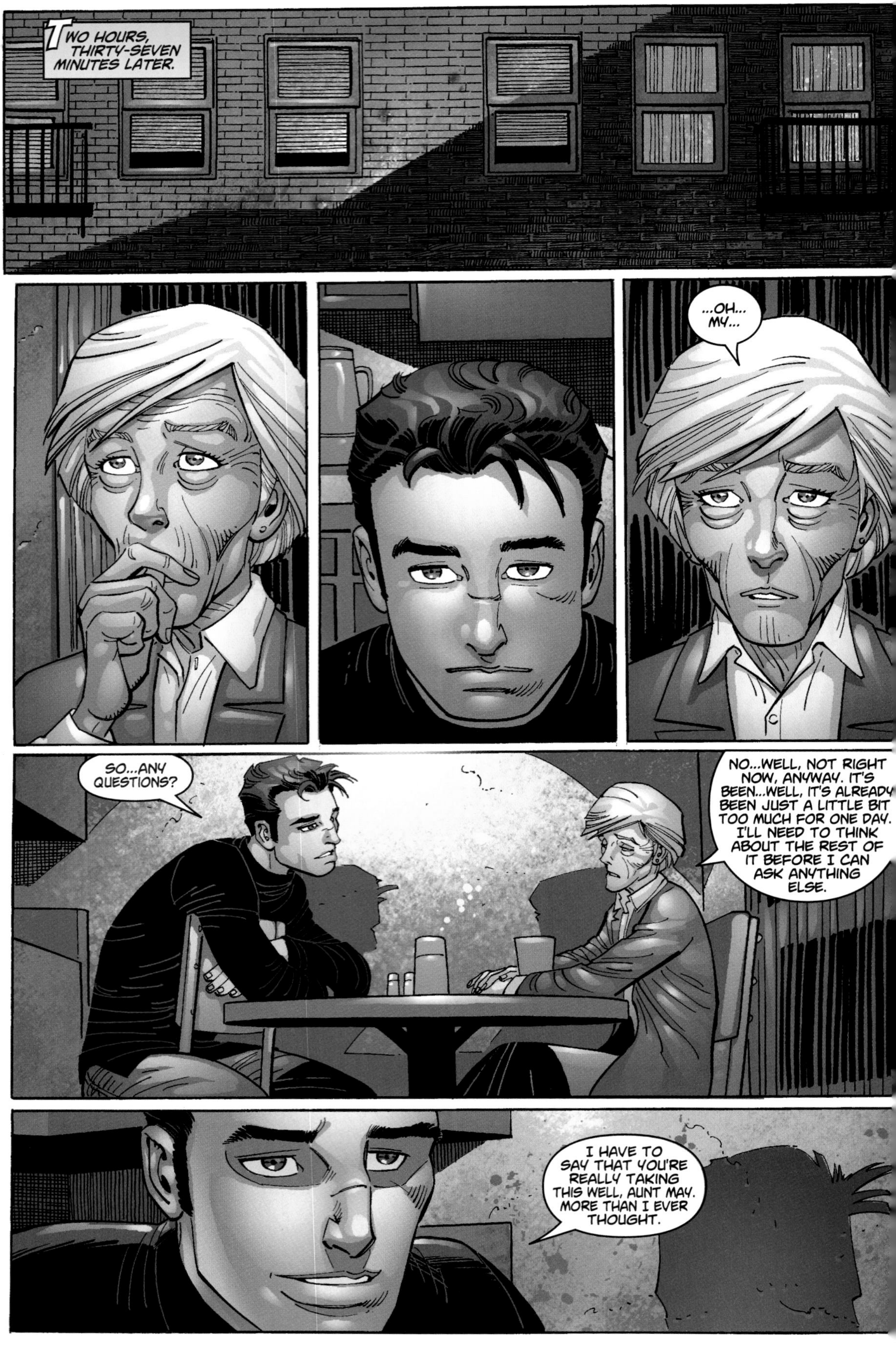
TWO HOURS, THIRTY-SEVEN MINUTES LATER.
...OH... MY...
SO...ANY QUESTIONS?
NO...WELL, NOT RIGHT NOW, ANYWAY. IT'S BEEN...WELL, IT'S ALREADY BEEN JUST A LITTLE BIT TOO MUCH FOR ONE DAY. I'LL NEED TO THINK ABOUT THE REST OF IT BEFORE I CAN ASK ANYTHING ELSE.
I HAVE TO SAY THAT YOU'RE REALLY TAKING THIS WELL, AUNT MAY. MORE THAN I EVER THOUGHT.

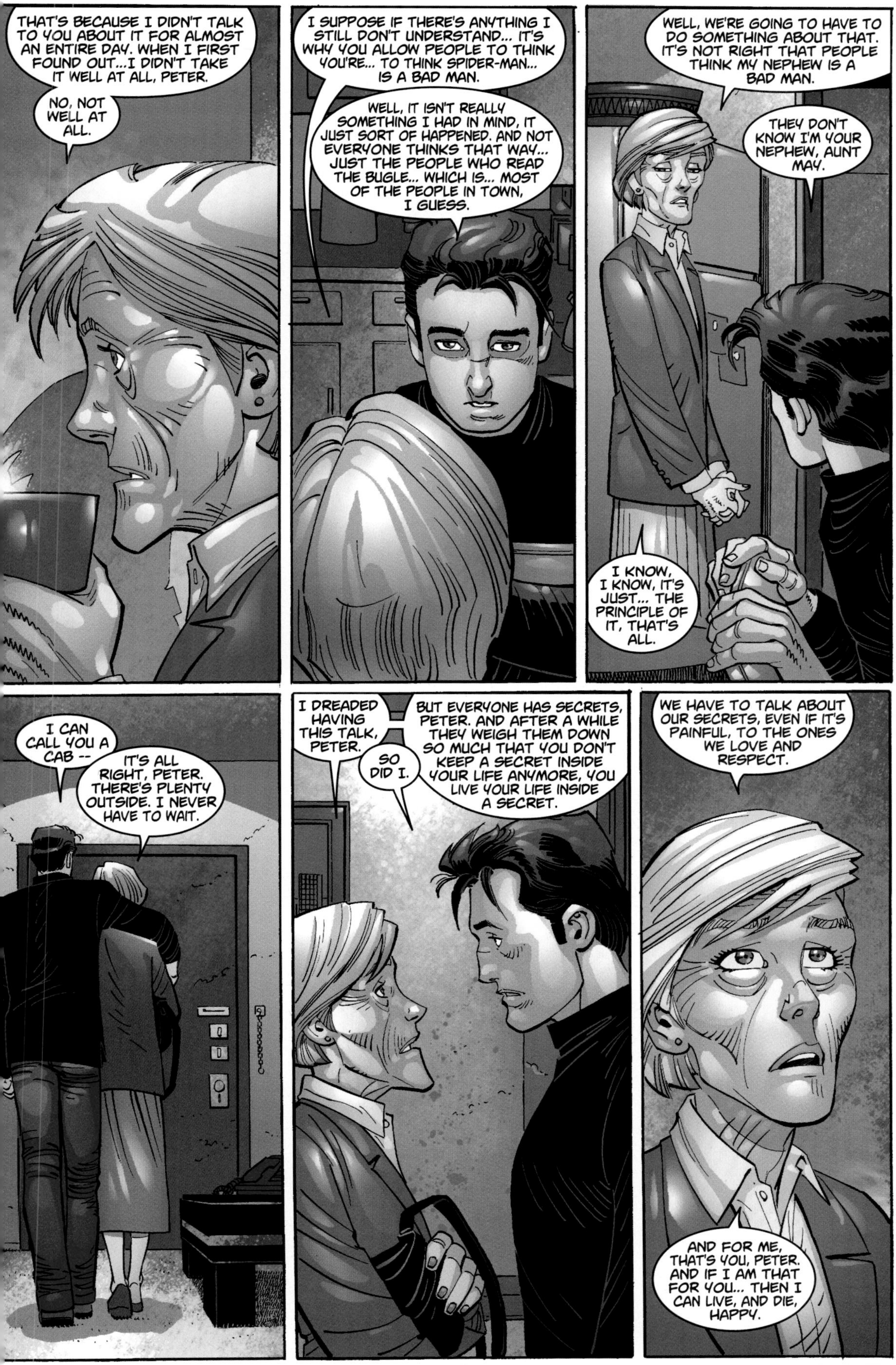
THAT'S BECAUSE I DIDN'T TALK TO YOU ABOUT IT FOR ALMOST AN ENTIRE DAY. WHEN I FIRST FOUND OUT...I DIDN'T TAKE IT WELL AT ALL, PETER.
NO, NOT WELL AT ALL.
I SUPPOSE IF THERE'S ANYTHING I STILL DON'T UNDERSTAND... IT'S WHY YOU ALLOW PEOPLE TO THINK YOU'RE... TO THINK SPIDER-MAN... IS A BAD MAN.
WELL, IT ISN'T REALLY SOMETHING I HAD IN MIND, IT JUST SORT OF HAPPENED. AND NOT EVERYONE THINKS THAT WAY... JUST THE PEOPLE WHO READ THE BUGLE... WHICH IS... MOST OF THE PEOPLE IN TOWN, I GUESS.
WELL, WE'RE GOING TO HAVE TO DO SOMETHING ABOUT THAT. IT'S NOT RIGHT THAT PEOPLE THINK MY NEPHEW IS A BAD MAN.
THEY DON'T KNOW I'M YOUR NEPHEW, AUNT MAY.
I KNOW, I KNOW, IT'S JUST... THE PRINCIPLE OF IT, THAT'S ALL.
I CAN CALL YOU A CAB --
IT'S ALL RIGHT, PETER. THERE'S PLENTY OUTSIDE. I NEVER HAVE TO WAIT.
I DREADED HAVING THIS TALK, PETER.
SO DID I.
BUT EVERYONE HAS SECRETS, PETER. AND AFTER A WHILE THEY WEIGH THEM DOWN SO MUCH THAT YOU DON'T KEEP A SECRET INSIDE YOUR LIFE ANYMORE, YOU LIVE YOUR LIFE INSIDE A SECRET.
WE HAVE TO TALK ABOUT OUR SECRETS, EVEN IF IT'S PAINFUL, TO THE ONES WE LOVE AND RESPECT.
AND FOR ME, THAT'S YOU, PETER. AND IF I AM THAT FOR YOU... THEN I CAN LIVE, AND DIE, HAPPY.

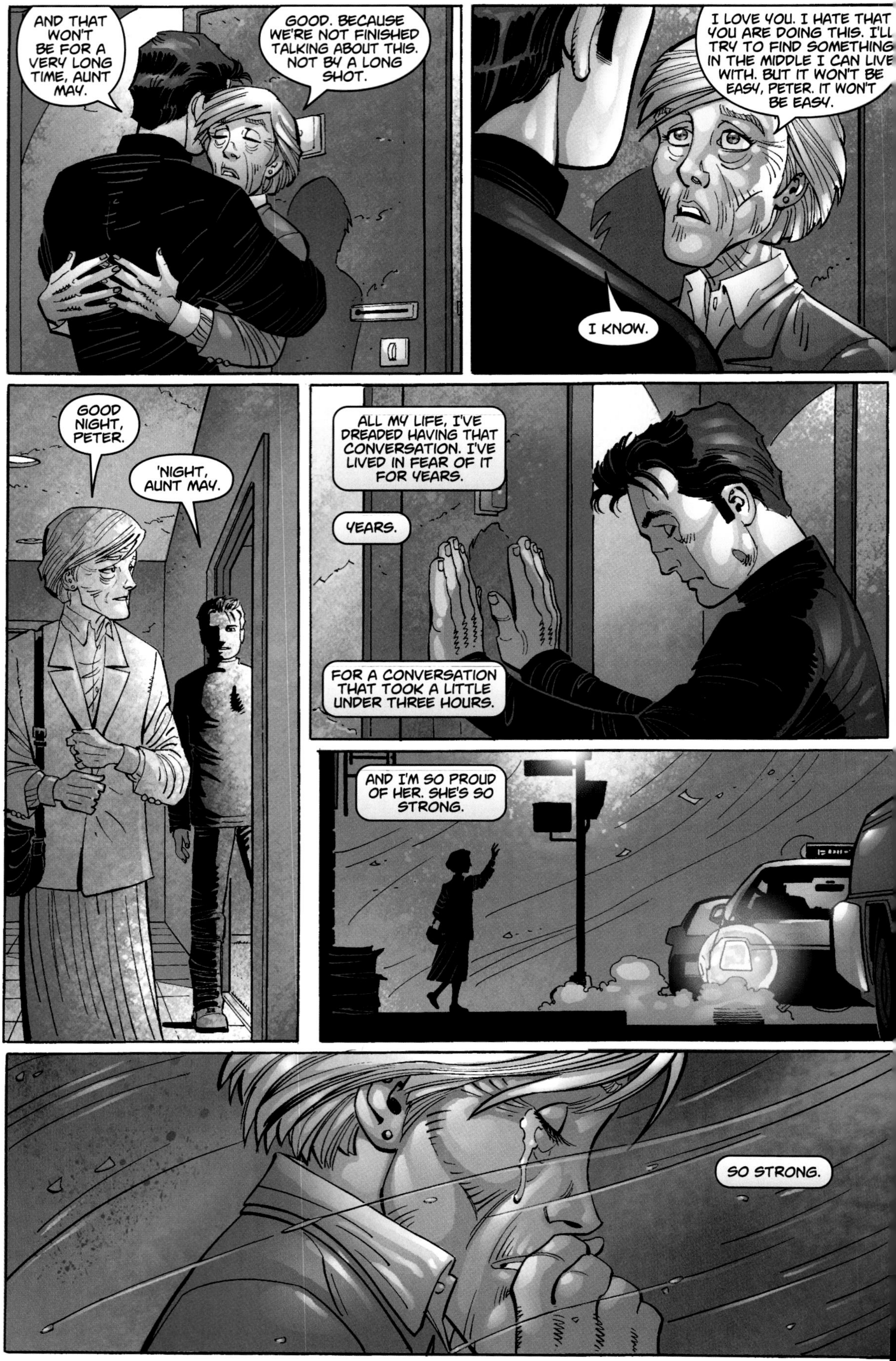
AND THAT WON'T BE FOR A VERY LONG TIME, AUNT MAY.
GOOD. BECAUSE WE'RE NOT FINISHED TALKING ABOUT THIS. NOT BY A LONG SHOT.
I LOVE YOU. I HATE THAT YOU ARE DOING THIS. I'LL TRY TO FIND SOMETHING IN THE MIDDLE I CAN LIVE WITH. BUT IT WON'T BE EASY, PETER. IT WON'T BE EASY.
I KNOW.
GOOD NIGHT, PETER.
'NIGHT, AUNT MAY.
ALL MY LIFE, I'VE DREADED HAVING THAT CONVERSATION. I'VE LIVED IN FEAR OF IT FOR YEARS.
YEARS.
FOR A CONVERSATION THAT TOOK A LITTLE UNDER THREE HOURS.
AND I'M SO PROUD OF HER. SHE'S SO STRONG.
SO STRONG.

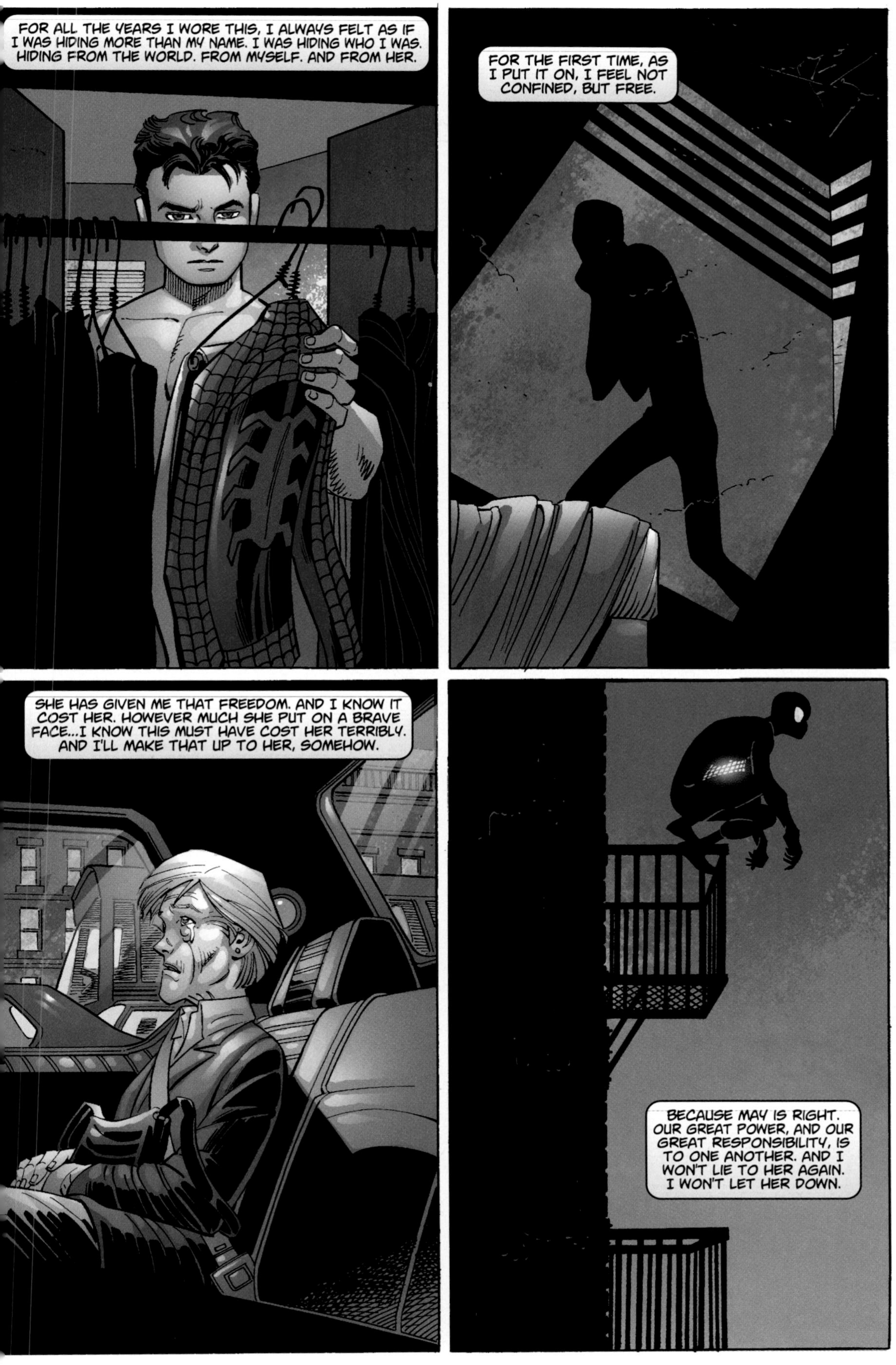
FOR ALL THE YEARS I WORE THIS, I ALWAYS FELT AS IF I WAS HIDING MORE THAN MY NAME. I WAS HIDING WHO I WAS. HIDING FROM THE WORLD. FROM MYSELF. AND FROM HER.
FOR THE FIRST TIME, AS I PUT IT ON, I FEEL NOT CONFINED, BUT FREE.
SHE HAS GIVEN ME THAT FREEDOM. AND I KNOW IT COST HER. HOWEVER MUCH SHE PUT ON A BRAVE FACE...I KNOW THIS MUST HAVE COST HER TERRIBLY. AND I'LL MAKE THAT UP TO HER, SOMEHOW.
BECAUSE MAY IS RIGHT. OUR GREAT POWER, AND OUR GREAT RESPONSIBILITY, IS TO ONE ANOTHER. AND I WON'T LIE TO HER AGAIN. I WON'T LET HER DOWN.

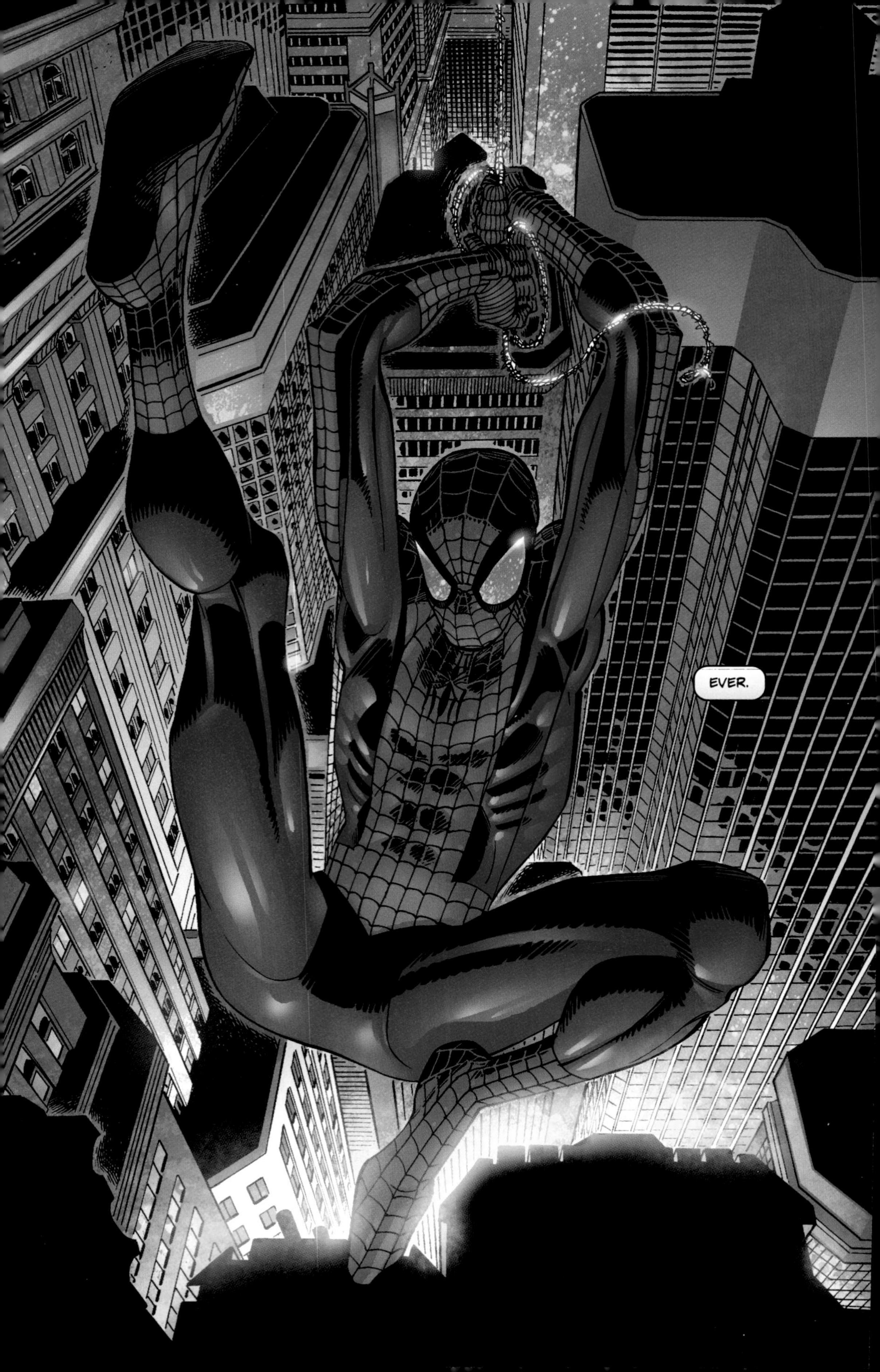
EVER.

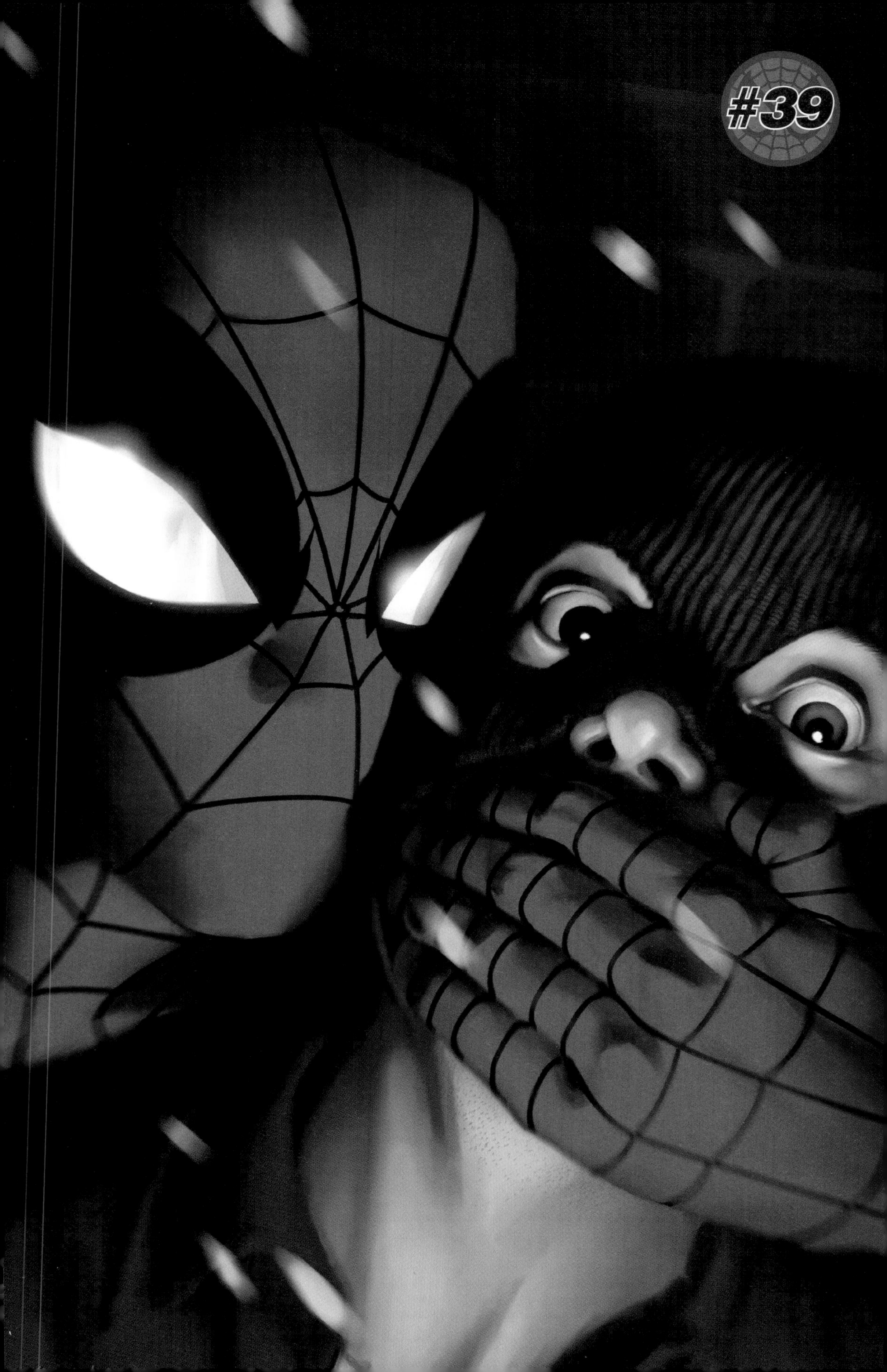
#39

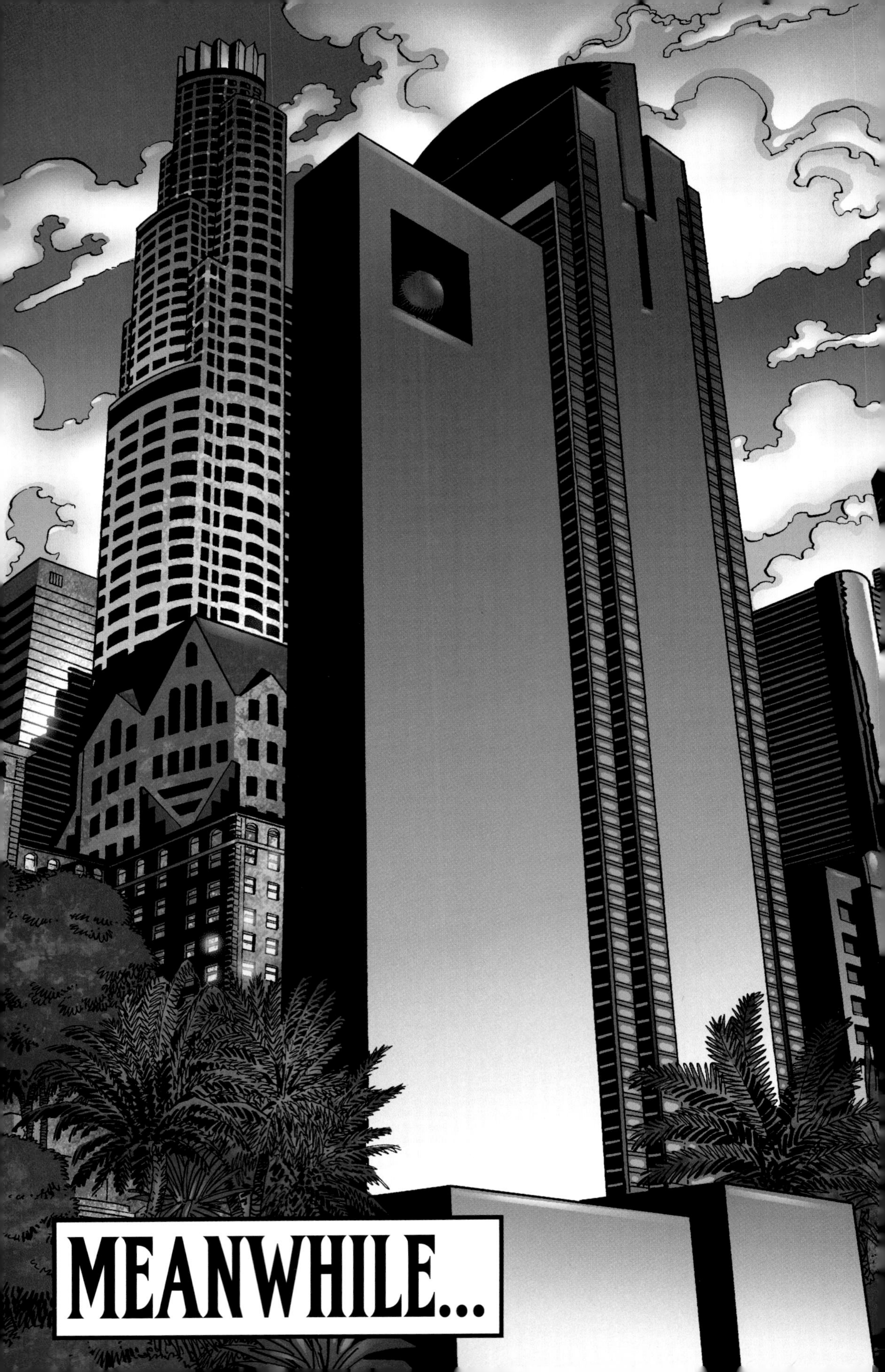
MEANWHILE...

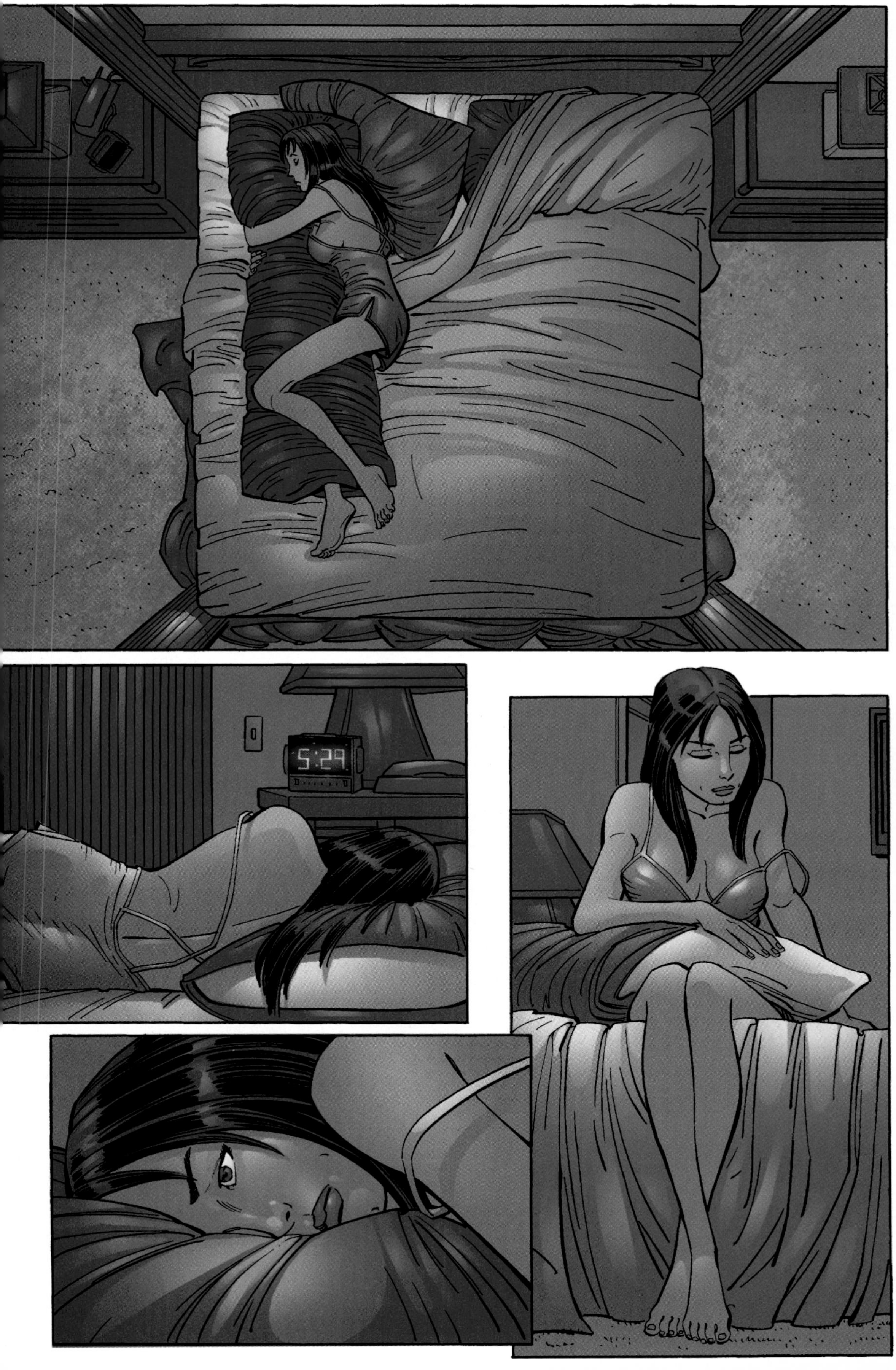
5:29

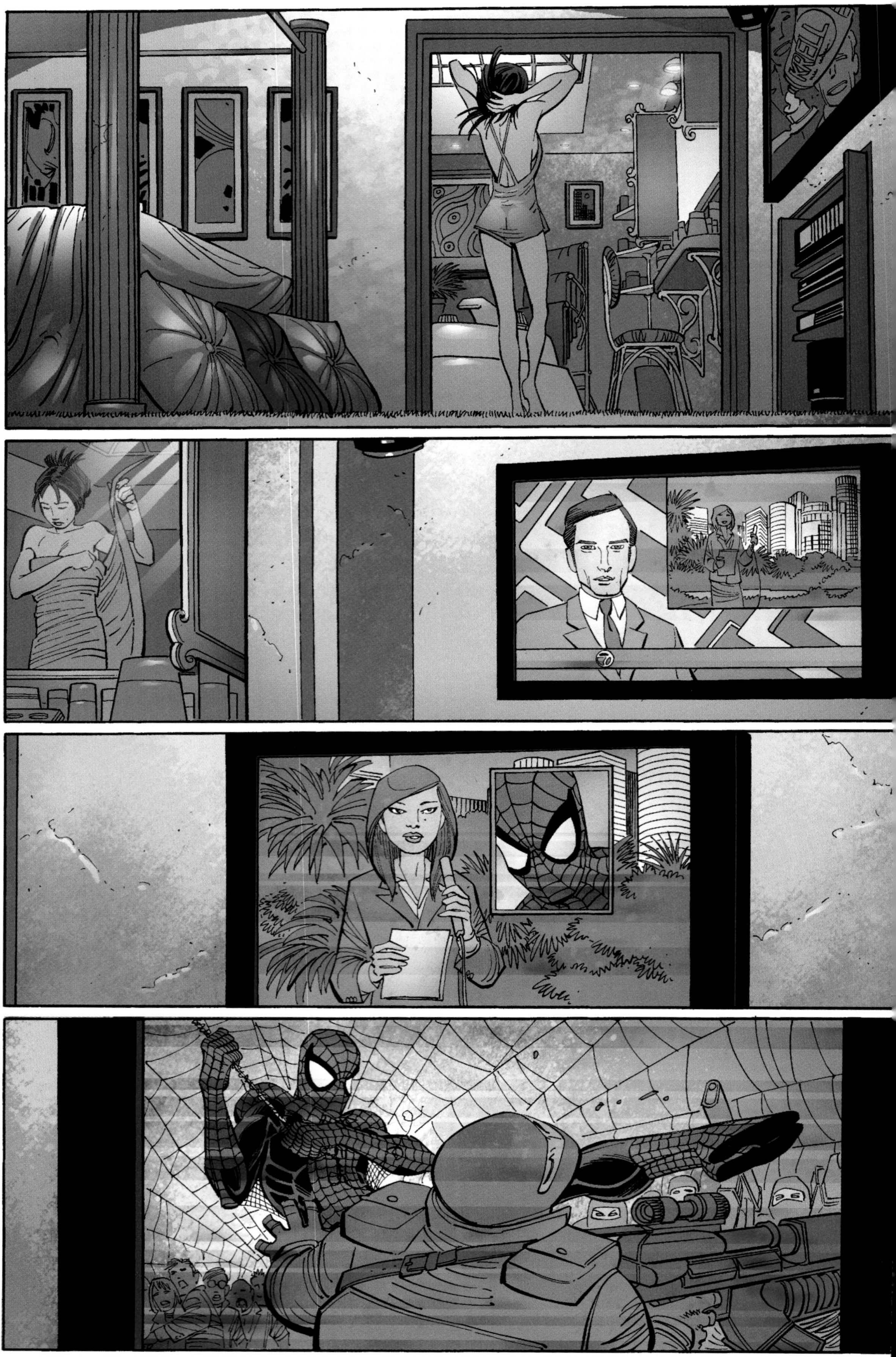

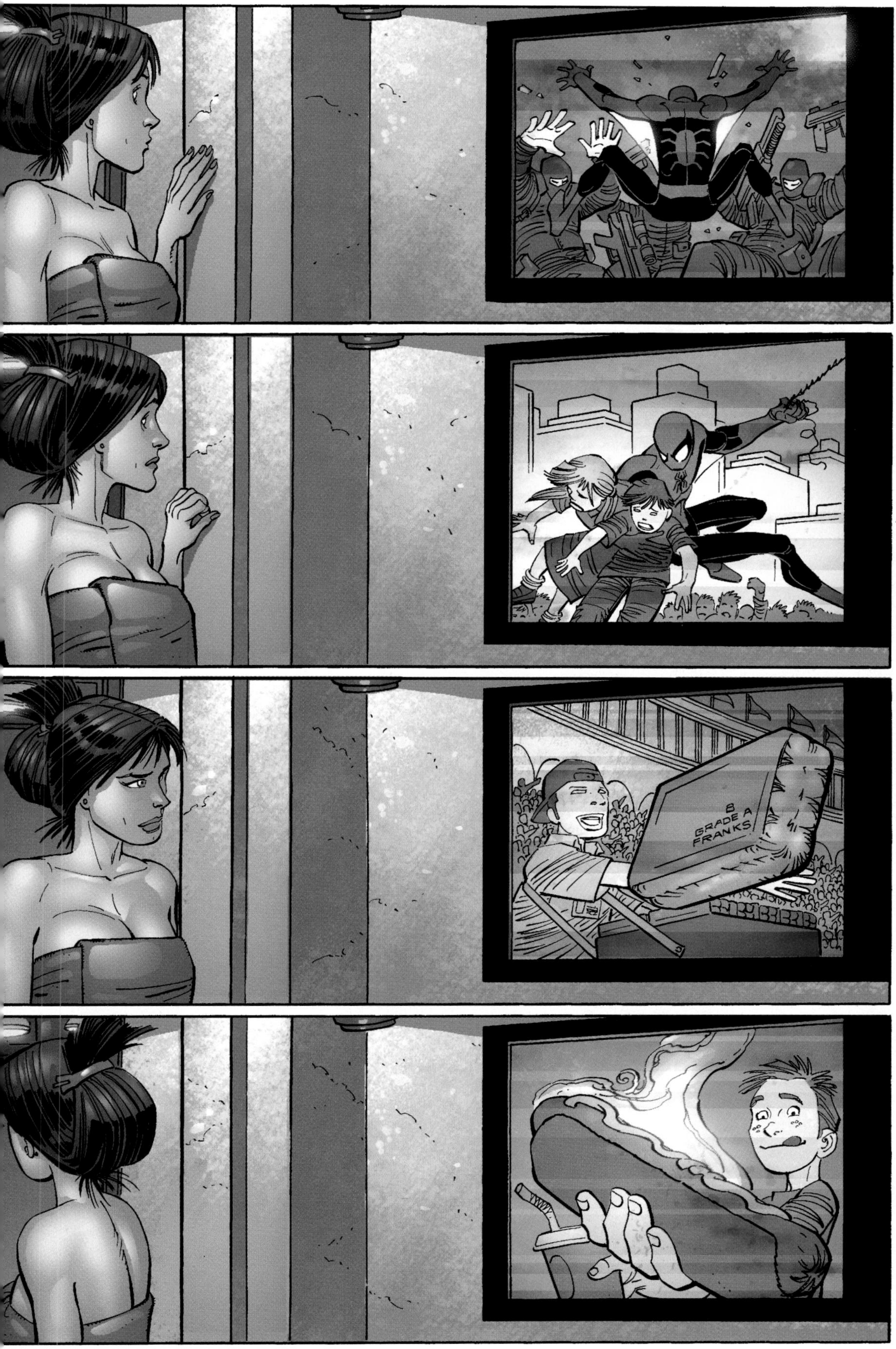
8
GRADE A
FRANKS

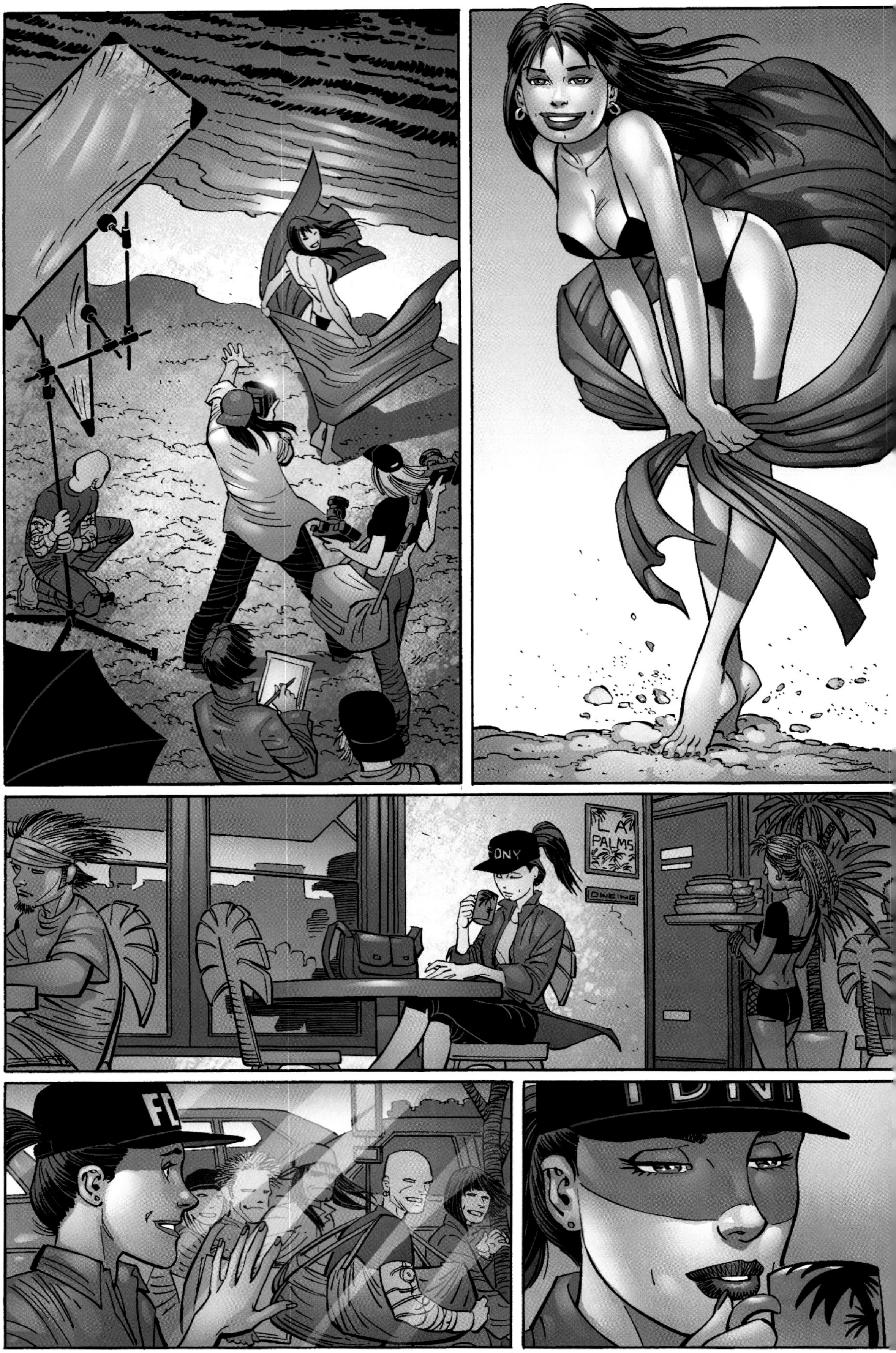
LA PALMS

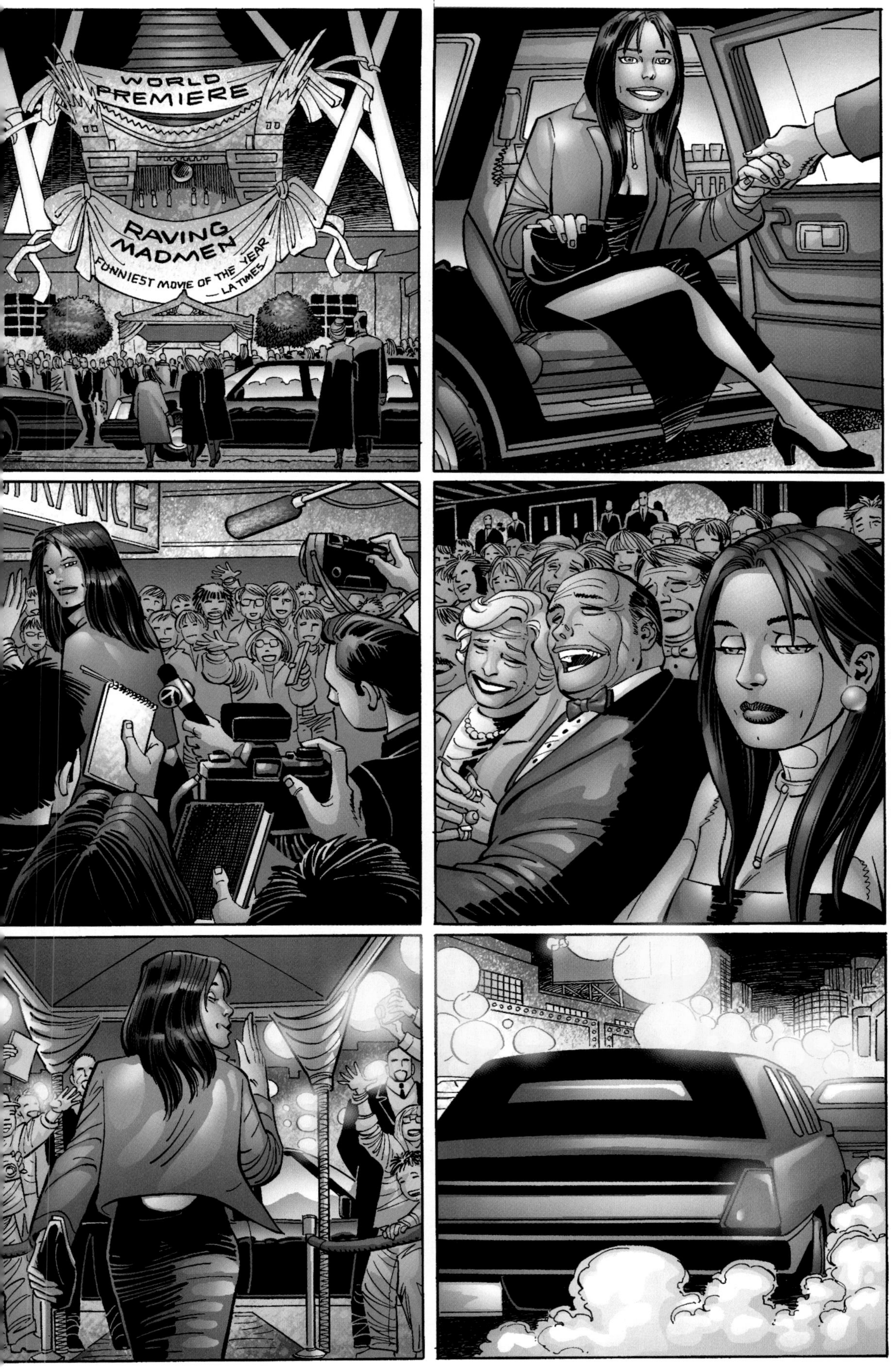
WORLD PREMIERE
RAVING MADMEN
FUNNIEST MOVIE OF THE YEAR
— LA TIMES

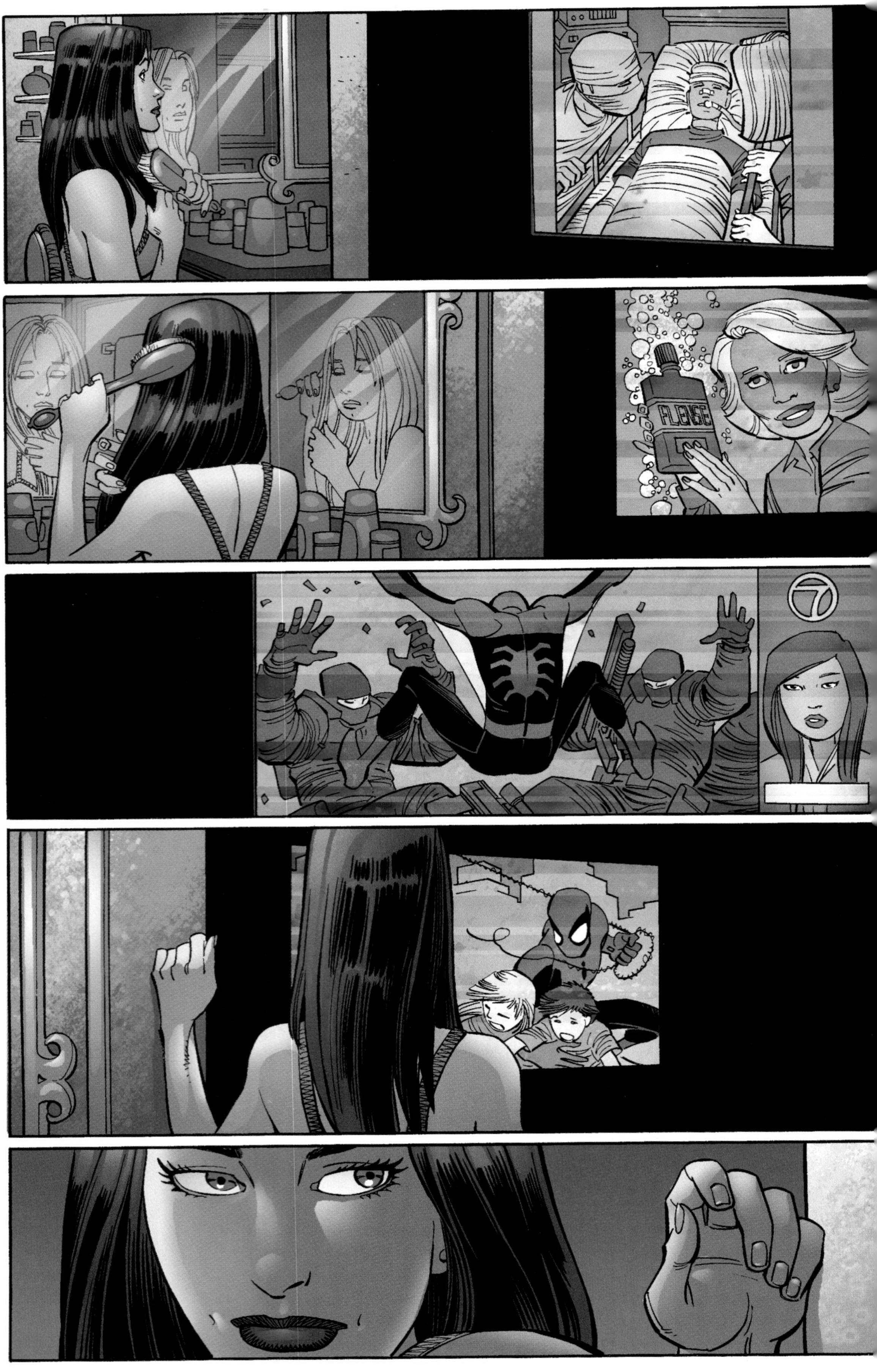
FLENGE

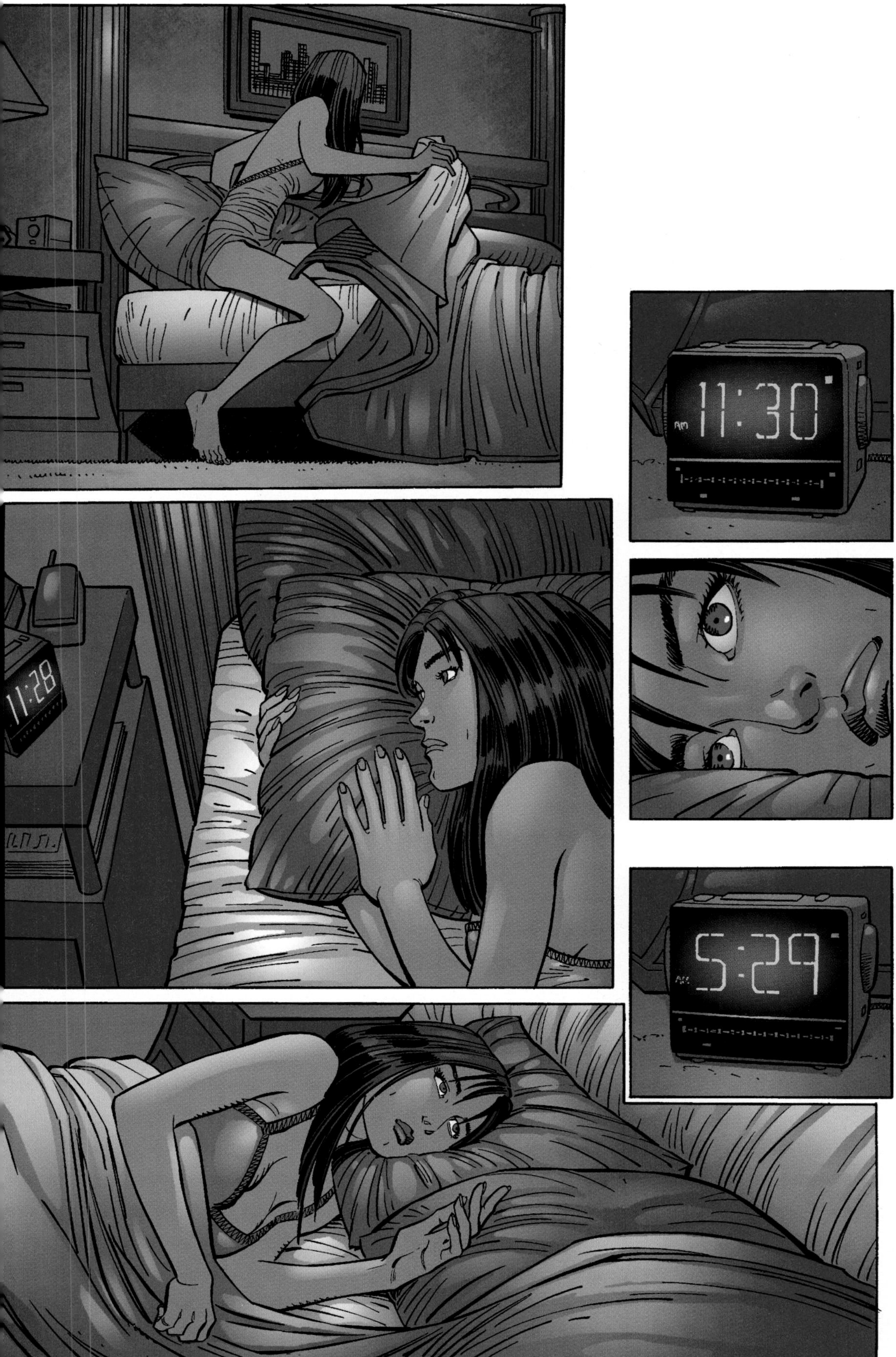
11:30
11:28
5:29

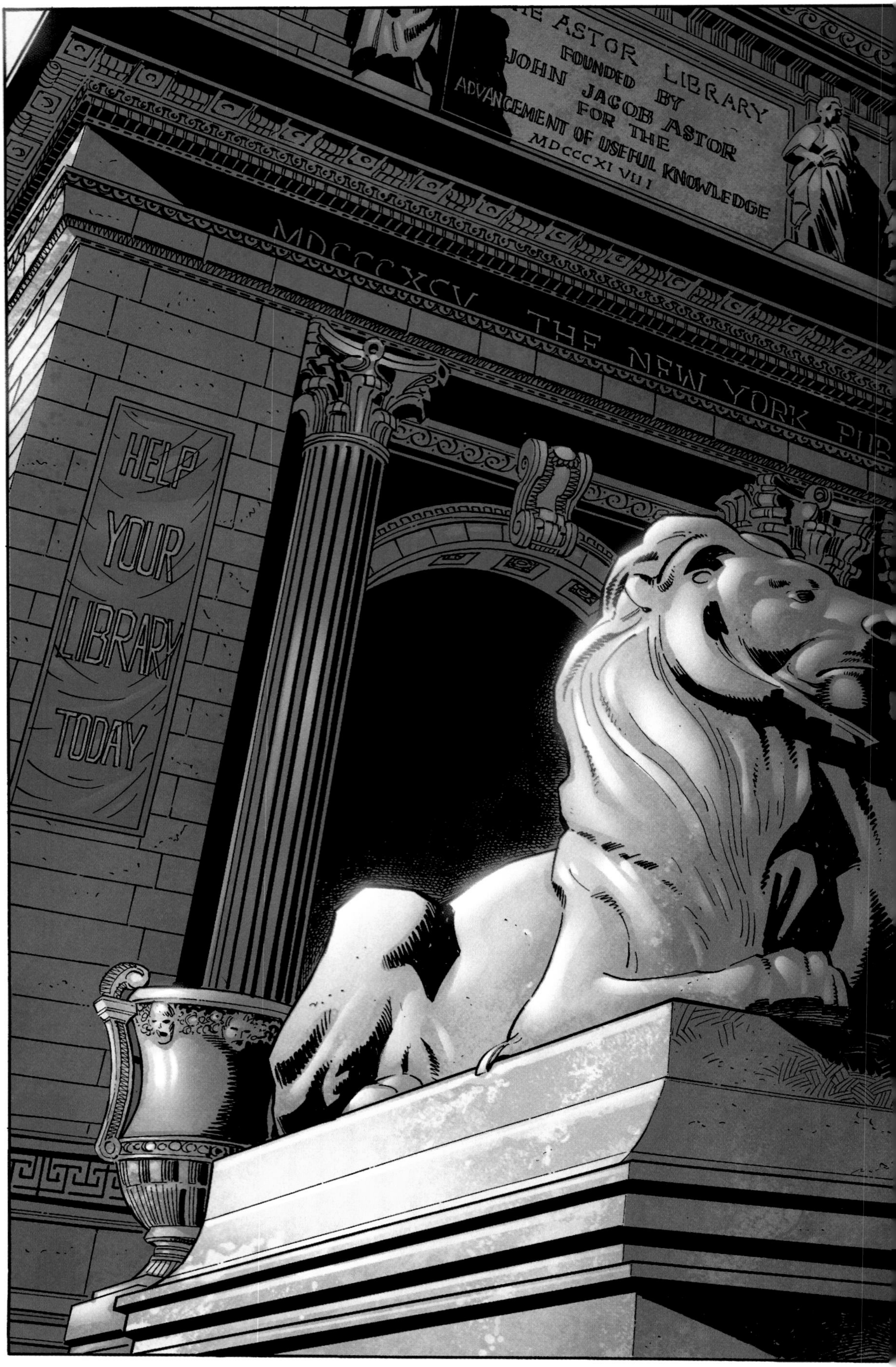
ASTOR LIBRARY
FOUNDED BY
JOHN JACOB ASTOR
FOR THE
ADVANCEMENT OF USEFUL KNOWLEDGE
MDCCCXI VIII
MDCCCXCV THE NEW YORK
HELP YOUR LIBRARY TODAY

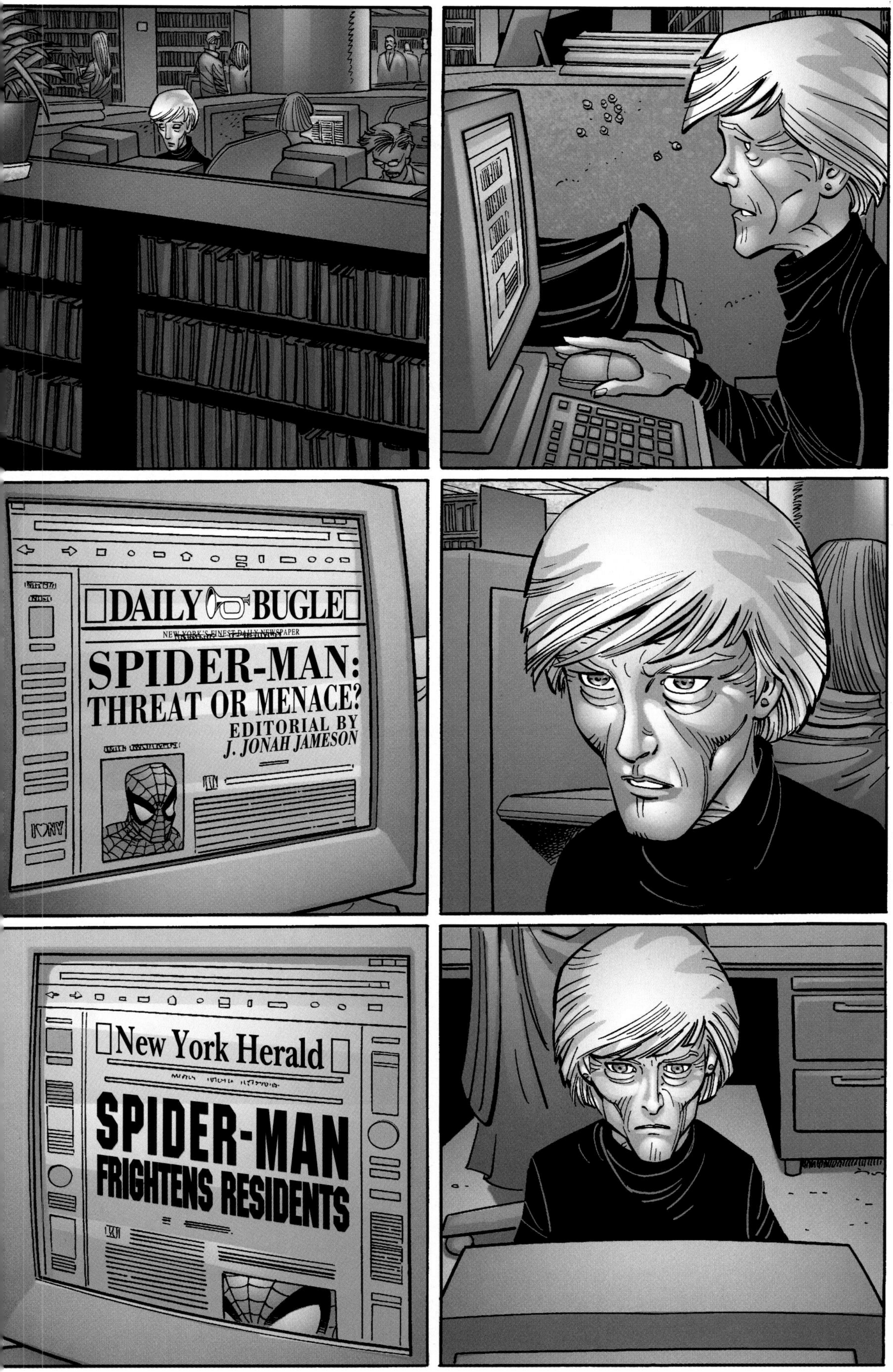
DAILY BUGLE
NEW YORK'S FINEST DAILY NEWSPAPER
SPIDER-MAN: THREAT OR MENACE?
EDITORIAL BY J. JONAH JAMESON
I ♥ NY
New York Herald
SPIDER-MAN FRIGHTENS RESIDENTS

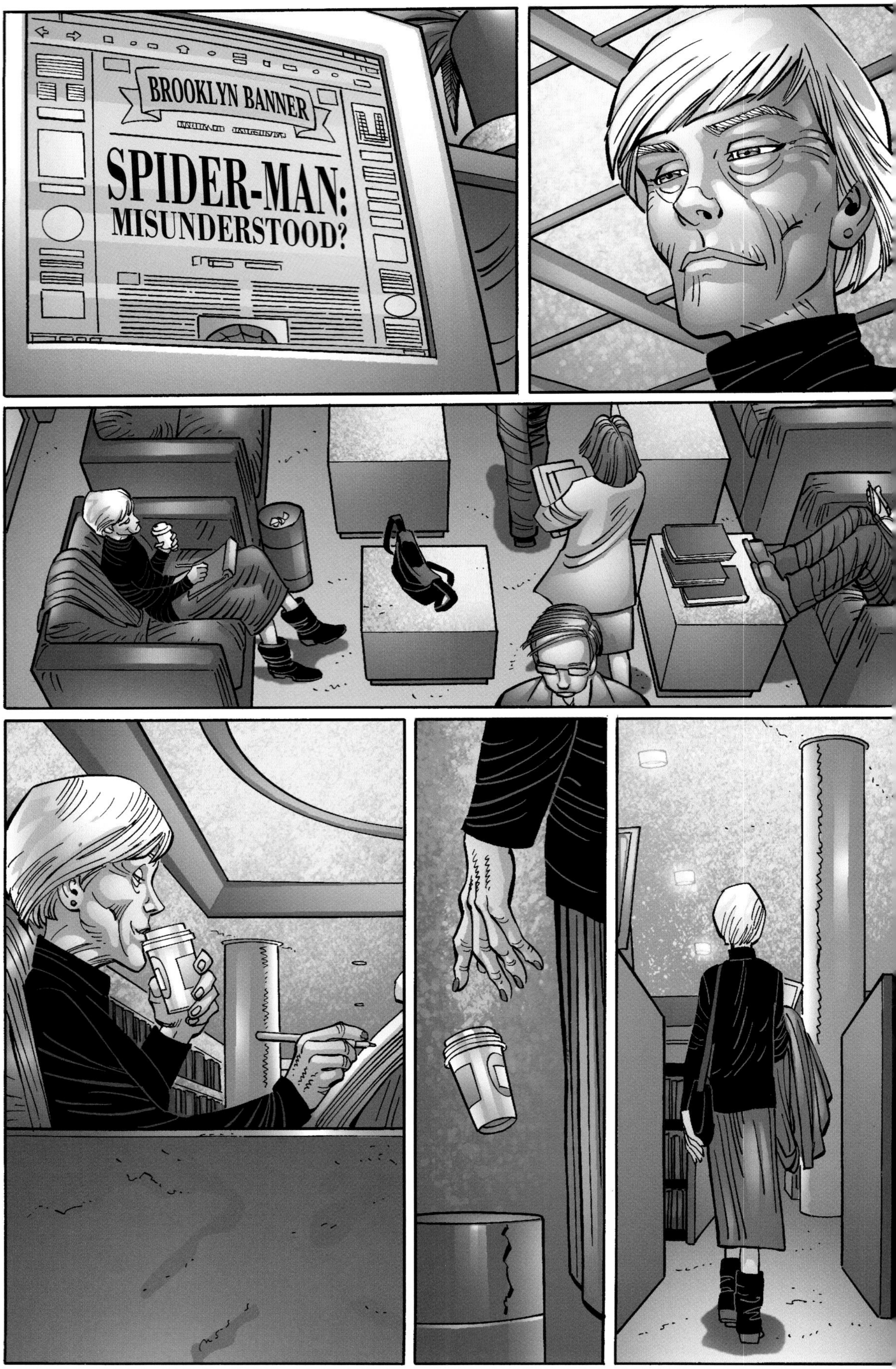

BROOKLYN BANNER
SPIDER-MAN:
MISUNDERSTOOD?

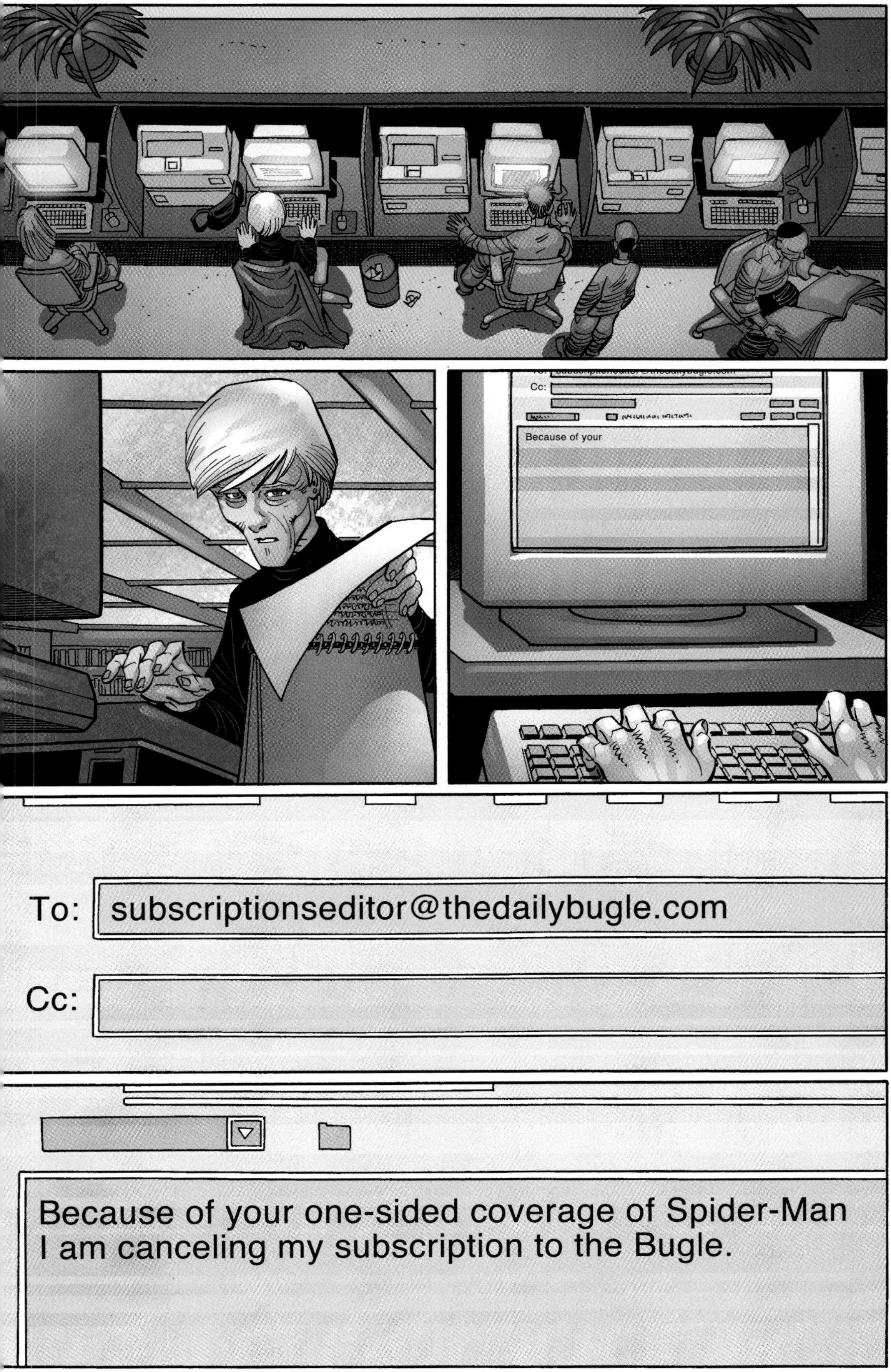
Cc:
Because of your
To: subscriptionseditor@thedailybugle.com
Cc:
Because of your one-sided coverage of Spider-Man
I am canceling my subscription to the Bugle.

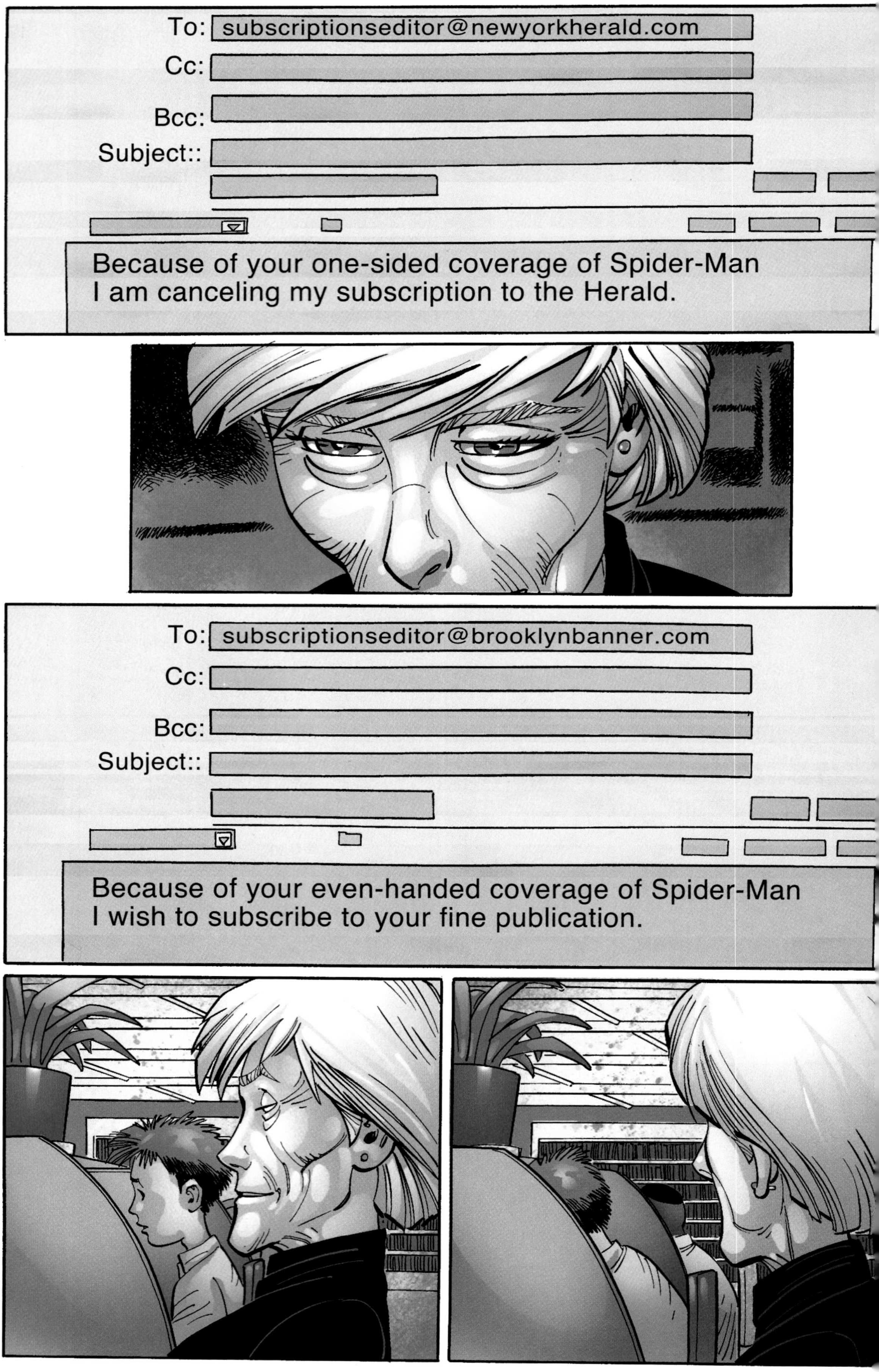
To: subscriptionseditor@newyorkherald.com
Cc:
Bcc:
Subject::
Because of your one-sided coverage of Spider-Man I am canceling my subscription to the Herald.
To: subscriptionseditor@brooklynbanner.com
Cc:
Bcc:
Subject::
Because of your even-handed coverage of Spider-Man I wish to subscribe to your fine publication.

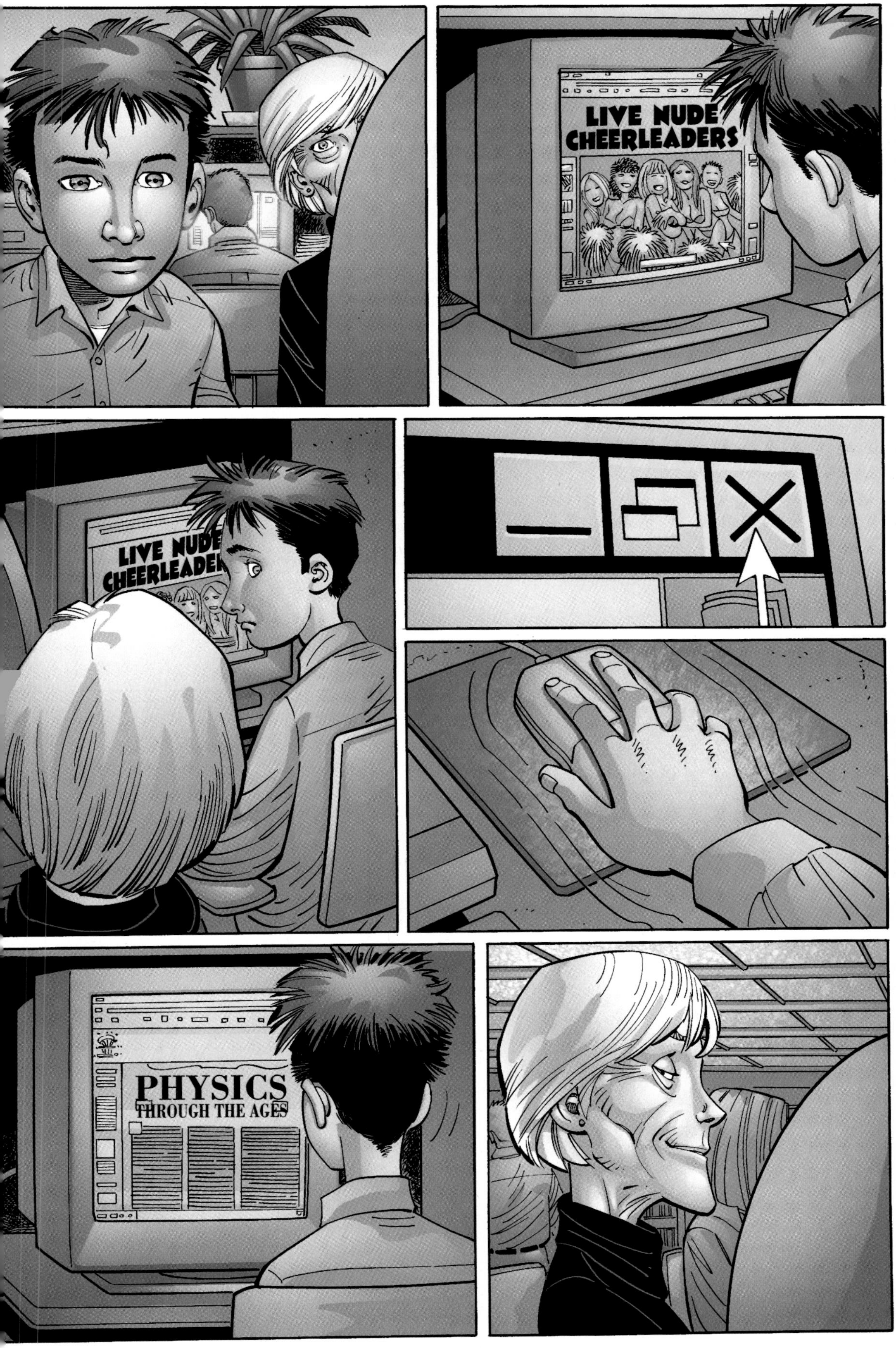

LIVE NUDE CHEERLEADERS
LIVE NUDE CHEERLEADERS
PHYSICS
THROUGH THE AGES

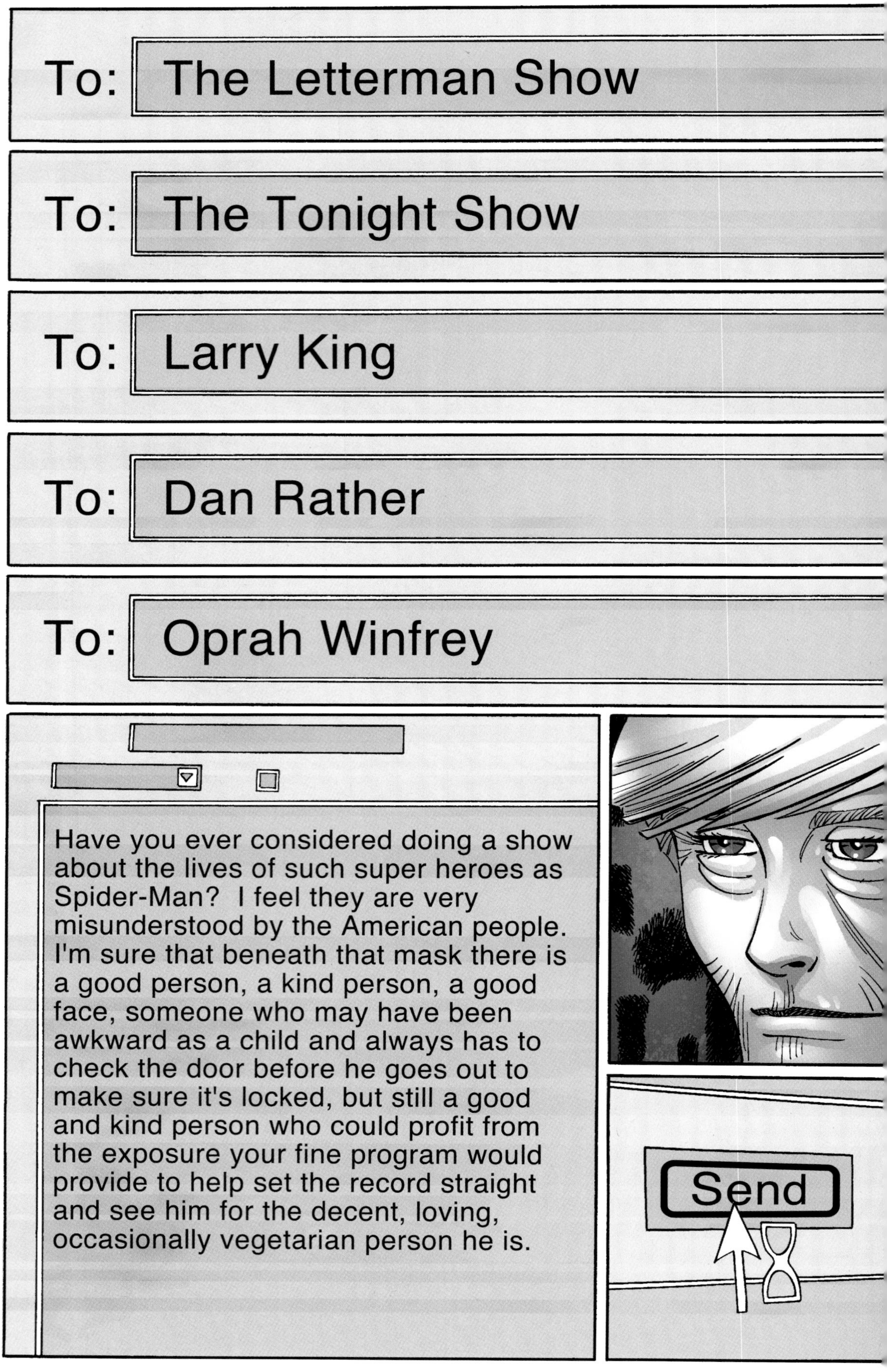
To: The Letterman Show
To: The Tonight Show
To: Larry King
To: Dan Rather
To: Oprah Winfrey
Have you ever considered doing a show about the lives of such super heroes as Spider-Man? I feel they are very misunderstood by the American people. I'm sure that beneath that mask there is a good person, a kind person, a good face, someone who may have been awkward as a child and always has to check the door before he goes out to make sure it's locked, but still a good and kind person who could profit from the exposure your fine program would provide to help set the record straight and see him for the decent, loving, occasionally vegetarian person he is.
Send

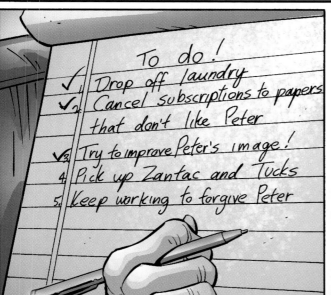

To do!
✓ 1. Drop off laundry
✓ 2. Cancel subscriptions to papers that don't like Peter
✓ 3. Try to improve Peter's image!
4. Pick up Zantac and Tucks
5. Keep working to forgive Peter

Keep working to forgive Peter

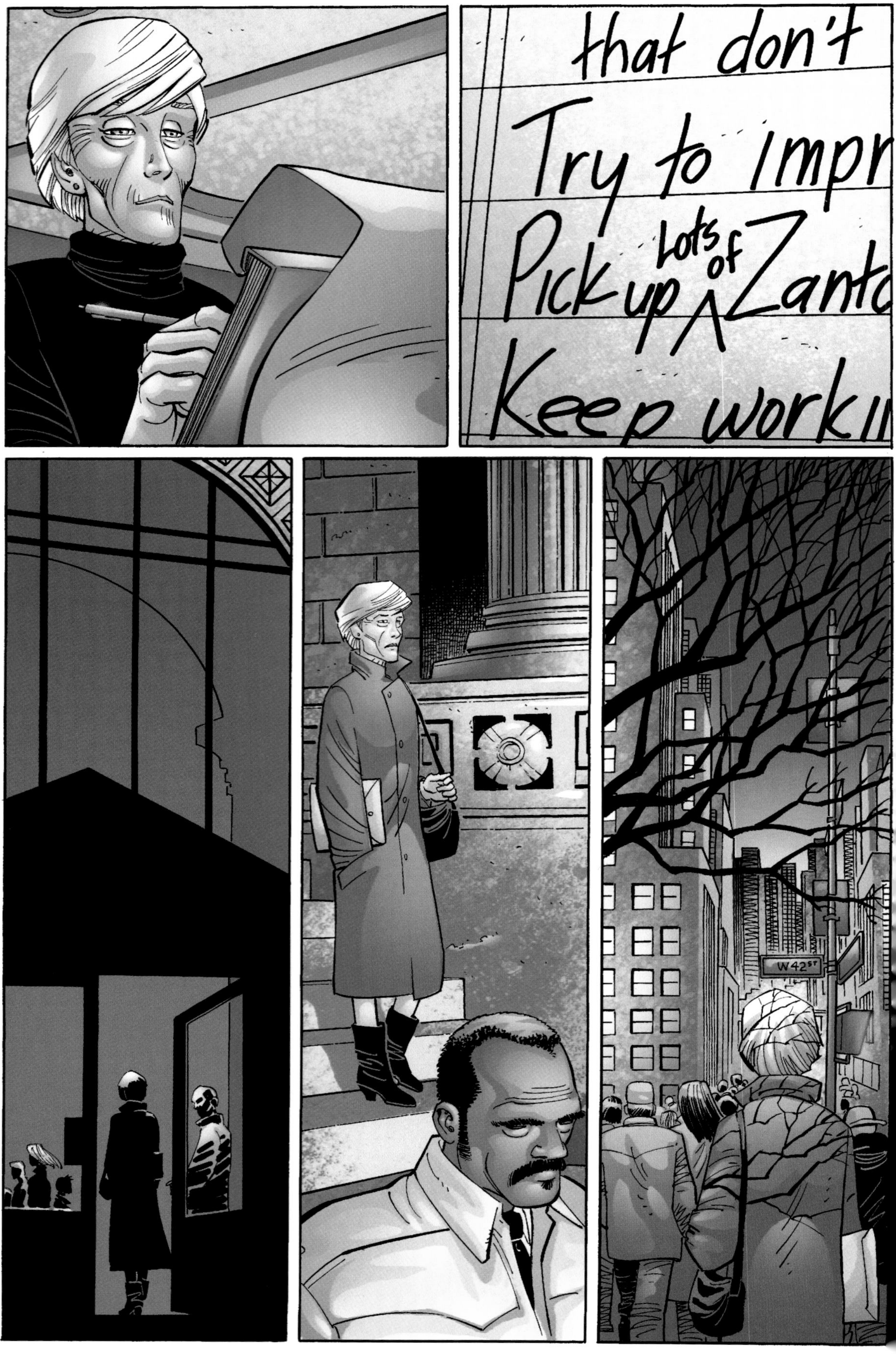

that don't
Try to impr
Pick up Lots of Zant
Keep worki
W 42ST

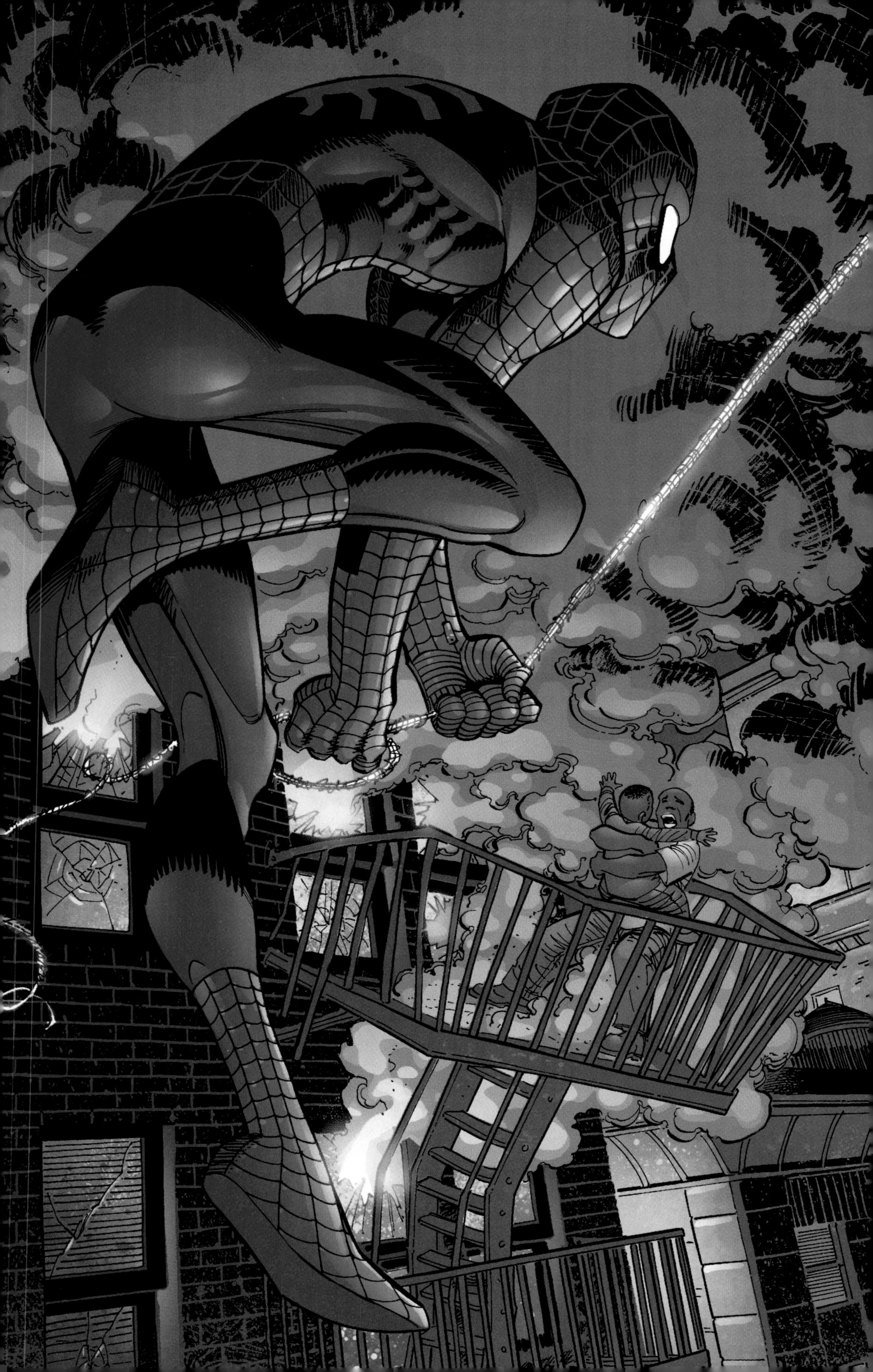

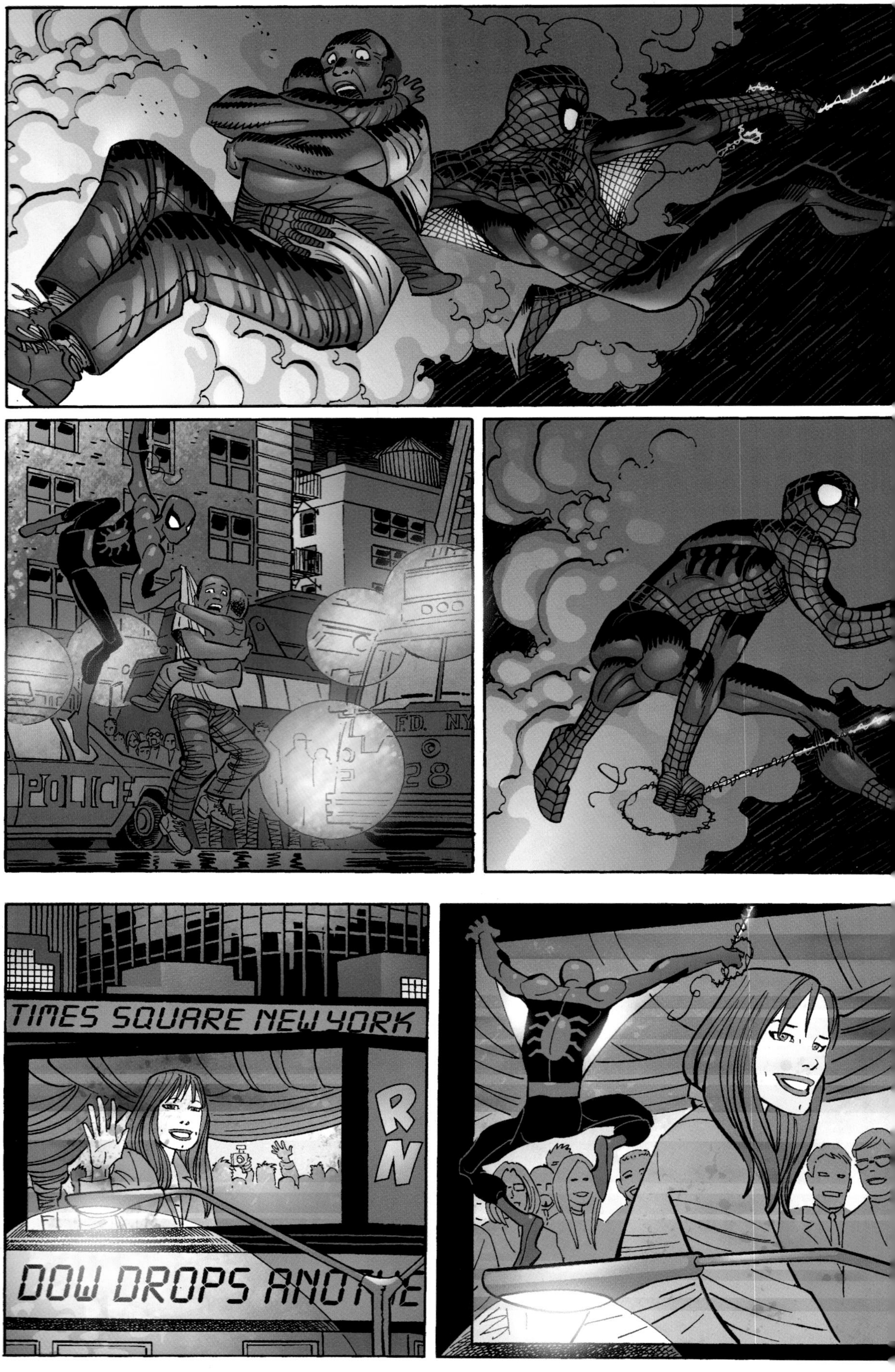

POLICE
F.D. N.Y
28
TIMES SQUARE NEW YORK
RN
DOW DROPS ANOTHE

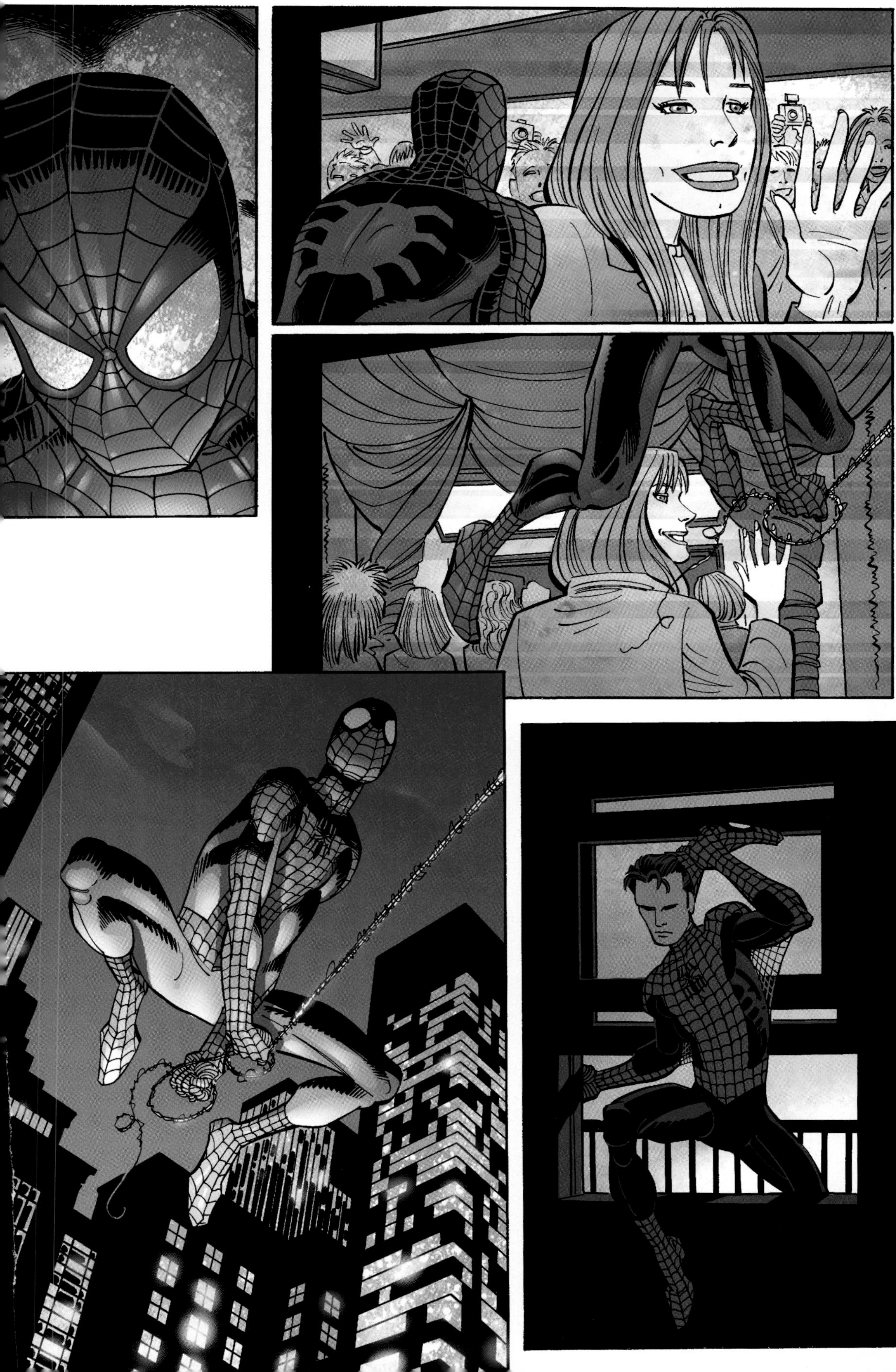

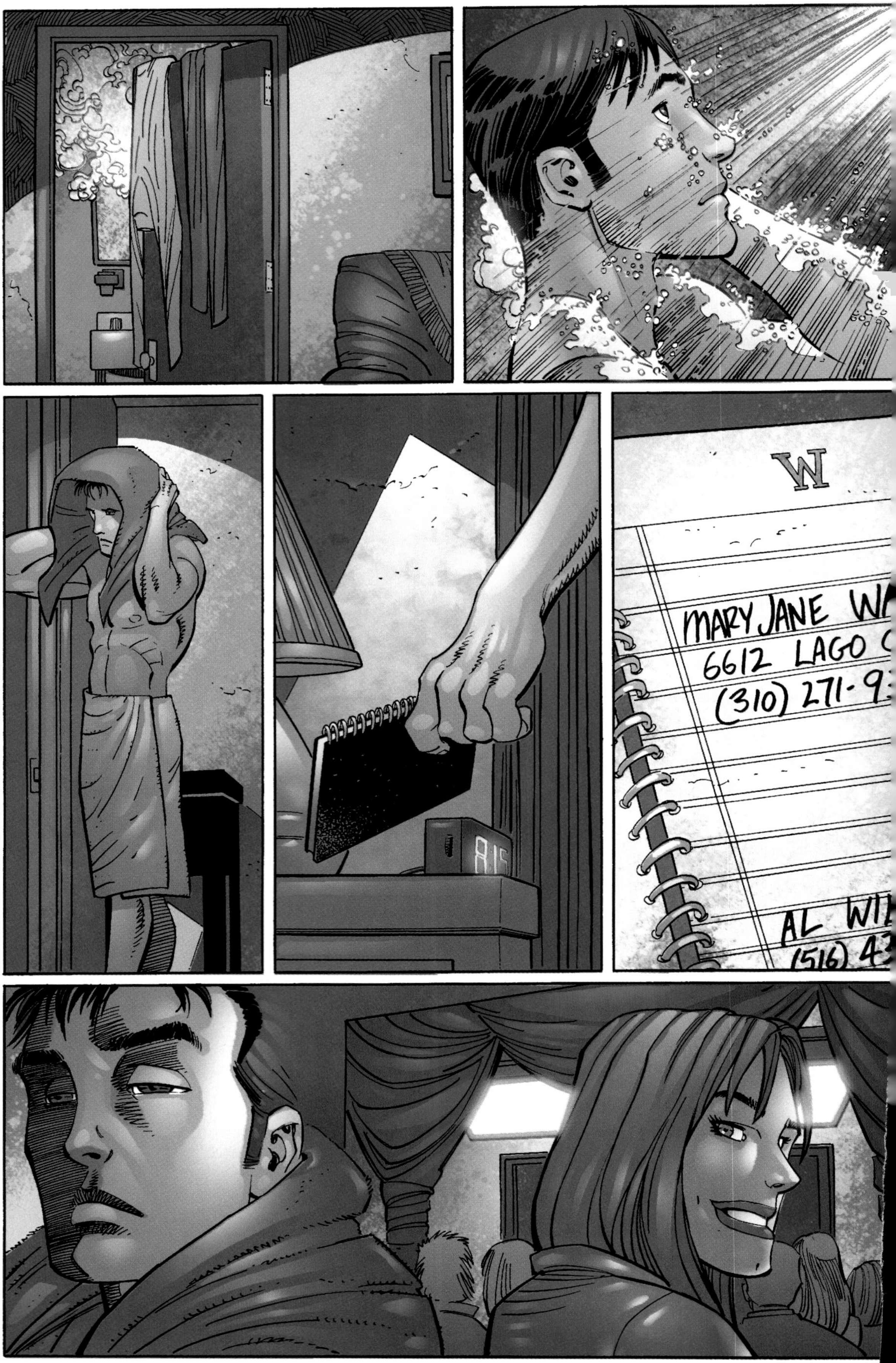

8:15
W
MARY JANE WA
6612 LAGO C
(310) 271-9
AL WI
(516) 43

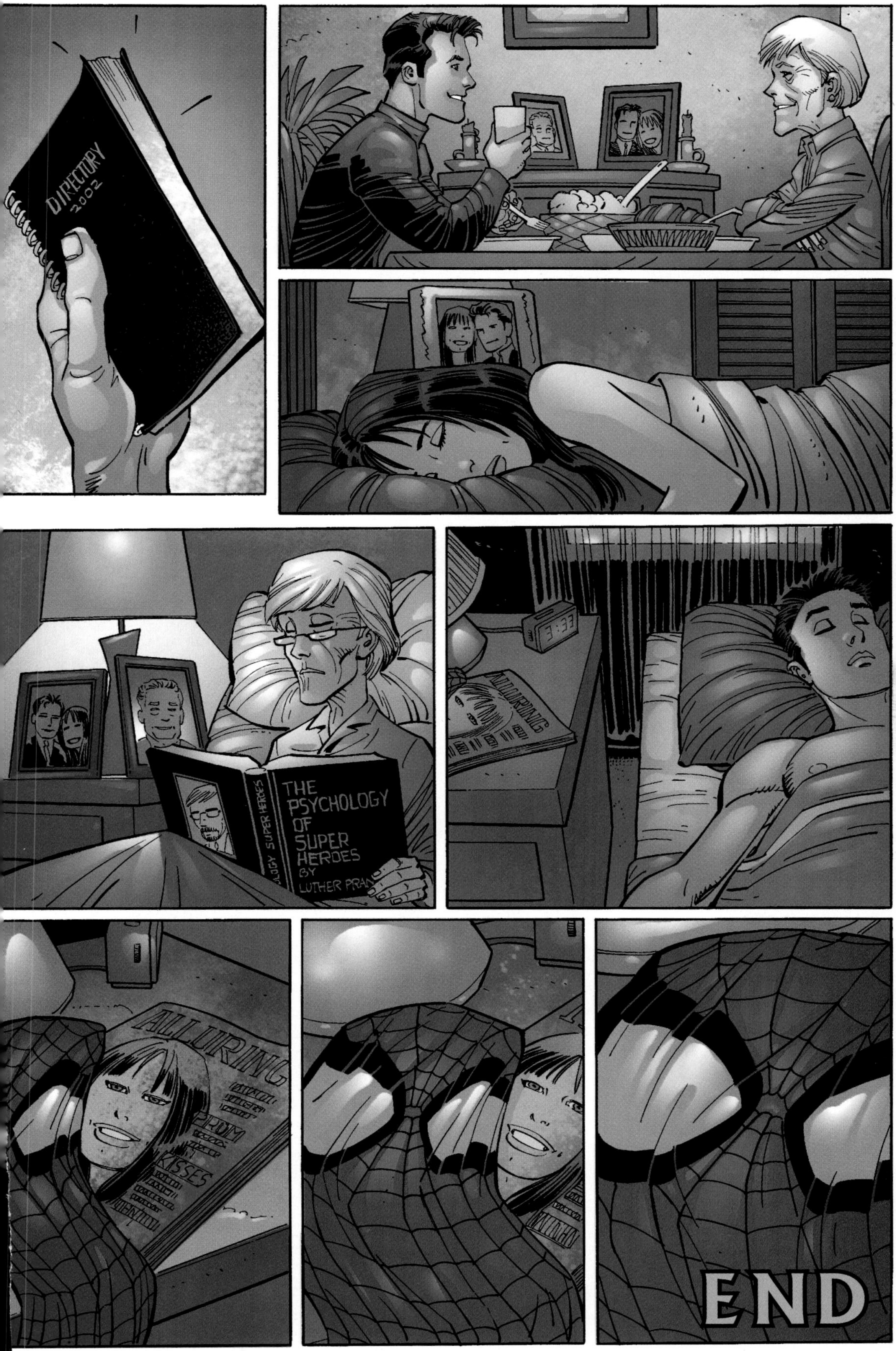

DIRECTORY
2002
THE PSYCHOLOGY OF SUPER HEROES
BY
LUTHER PRAN
ALLURING
PROM
KISSES
END